For my beautiful daughter Bridget, who reminds me to laugh and savor the simple things that make each day special. My greatest hope in life is to inspire her to live out her wildest dreams.

STAND OUT FROM THE REST OF THE CROWD

BUILDING BRAND [YOU]™

*be relevant.
or be replaceable.*

CYNDEE WOOLLEY

Copyright © 2013 by C2 Communications, LLC

Published by BrandPro Media LLC

All rights reserved. No part of this book may be reproduced in any manner whatsoever without written permission, except in the case of brief quotations embodied in critical articles and reviews.

Cover design and interior layout by www.PearCreative.ca

Printed in the U.S.A

ISBN 978-0-9913751-0-3

TABLE OF CONTENTS

CHAPTER ONE   23
    It all begins with a brand

CHAPTER TWO   34
    Breaking trust will break your brand

CHAPTER THREE   40
    1. You are Brand [You]

CHAPTER FOUR   47
    Gain perspective on Brand [You]

CHAPTER FIVE   52
    2. Set your sights and your goals for [You]topia

CHAPTER SIX   67
    Aligning your priorities with [You]topia

CHAPTER SEVEN   75
    What are your values?

CHAPTER EIGHT   84
    Set your goals to achieve your [You]topia

CHAPTER NINE   95
    3. Value Brand [You] or no one else will

CHAPTER TEN   110
    4. Build your network wisely

CHAPTER ELEVEN   131
    5. Brand [You] must be simple, short and strong

CHAPTER TWELVE   158
    6. Smart brands speak up

CHAPTER THIRTEEN   181
    7. Be relevant or be replaceable

CHAPTER FOURTEEN 191
  Conclusion
ACKNOWLEDGEMENTS 198
ABOUT THE AUTHOR 199
REFERENCES 200

CONTRIBUTING THOUGHT LEADER

This book would not have been possible without the contributions of an amazing woman, business professional, thought leader and friend, Jessica Macera. Together, we spent countless hours drinking coffee, debating brands, and developing our own goals.

[Jessica Macera, MBA] [Cyndee Woolley, APR]

Jessica Macera, MBA is a business management consultant and a partner in Business Dynamix Solutions. She has extensive experience in operations management and strategic planning. Her passion is developing methods for small business owners to enhance business efficiency and profitability. Macera was recognized as one of the American Business Women's Association 2012 National Top Ten Businesswomen for professional contributions and civic involvement.

FOREWORD

I'm passionate about what I do. I love life, with all of the possibilities and experiences it offers.

I have a reputation for living life outside the traditional lines that many people follow. Some call me passionate, driven, or intense, but probably my favorite is "unbridled".

To me, unbridled means I'm in control of my future and nothing can hold me back.

While I will never be able to have power over the "things" that happen around me, I can still shape my own future because I've taken the time to identify what is important to me and build my personal brand around the things I love.

Because I have confidence in my brand, it helps me cut through the clutter life throws at me and set the tone and pace for where I want to go. It gives me the freedom to choose the right path for me.

Knowing I have power over my future gives me great comfort because the life I choose is an exciting and fulfilling one.

Once you've finished Building Brand [You], you will also be ready to choose your path and run full-speed ahead, unbridled and free of the reigns that hold others back from true success.

Cyndee Woolley

INTRODUCTION

Building your personal brand will help you work smarter, make more money and live out your wildest dreams.

In this book, I will share with you the process of personal branding I have developed by incorporating seven lessons learned from some of our nation's top brands, years of experience as a public relations professional and my own experience laying the framework for my own brand and launching my business.

You already have a brand

Whether you realize it or not, whether you believe it or not, you already have a brand. Too often, professionals allow their brands to be shaped by unfocused and haphazard responses to the circumstances surrounding them.

By going through the process of identifying and building your personal brand, you are transforming a de facto brand into exactly what you need to reach your goals.

You are building Brand [You].

When is the right time to build Brand [You]?

So many Americans have had their lives rocked by, well, life in general. You make plans, start a family, start a career; and sometimes life gets in the way. Something shifts and knocks you off-balance.

- Maybe you've started a career and, when the economy shifted, you lost your job.

- Maybe you placed your career on hold to start a family and need to re-enter the workforce, but your job is now obsolete.

- Maybe you've always dreamed of starting a business, but held on to the steady income of a less-than-ideal job because other priorities were your main concern.

- Maybe your whole world has shifted because of a major illness or divorce.

- Maybe you are feeling "stuck" in general, wishing you were able to live out a bigger purpose and leave your mark on this world.

- Or, maybe you are just exhausted from the twelve-hour days, the increasing demands of your job, the constant buzzing of your smartphone and the pressure to always be "on".

If you are nodding your head in agreement to any of the statements above, you have lost control of Brand [You]. Chances are, you are spending more time responding to other people's needs and life's circumstances than actively pursuing your dreams. While your dreams and projects remain half-started, you find yourself racing to put out someone else's fire.

The absolute best time to build Brand [You] is before you need it. With a confident brand in place, chances are good that you won't be the one who is laid off because your employers will know exactly how valuable you are.

If you do find yourself among the unlucky few who lose their jobs, you will have a network of contacts who are ready to snatch you up as soon as you hit the market because of your value.

However, if you are among the many Americans who are unsettled in their careers, unhappy with the direction their careers are taking or dreaming of starting a business, you need to start working on your brand immediately so that you can pull yourself up and put your life on track.

In today's tumultuous times

Whether you call a multinational corporation or a local retail shop your work home, a vibrant and positive personal brand is vital to your success. Why? These days, your career success depends almost entirely on you.

The definition of a successful career has evolved through the years. Decades ago, getting a job with a prominent company like IBM, AT&T, General Motors, or Procter & Gamble provided you with the long-term security of a good benefits package and pension plan.

You paid your dues by showing up and doing a decent job so that you would probably advance through the ranks and earn modest pay increases.

The comfortable corporate environment that allowed you to "pass Go" and collect your annual bonuses has disappeared. The shifting economy and the evolving motivations of consumers have rocked corporations. Even those who depended on the security of a government job are watching their benefits packages get whittled away.

Now, even if you work for Google or Whole Foods, your job security isn't measured by your satisfactory performance and tenure with the company. Your job security is measured by your observed ability to deliver results that improve the company's top- and bottom-line performance.

But without a memorable personal brand, how will your supervisor, your colleagues, or the management team know exactly how valuable you are, let alone WHO you are?

Even if you have a solid relationship with your existing supervisor, your supervisor is not guaranteed to be there for you tomorrow. Your boss' position is just as fluid as yours.

You need to build a broad network of support so that your accomplishments are well-known throughout your company and in your industry. Upon meeting you, a colleague or client should quickly understand who you are and what you can do. They need to know Brand [You].

If people don't know who you are or what you have to offer, you are expendable. In accounting terms, you are a potential liability instead of a valued asset. When it is time to cut expenses, you are among the rest of the "liabilities" placed on the chopping block.

The bottom line is: If you aren't actively building Brand [You], you are Brand [Screwed].

My first lesson in the value of a personal brand

Fresh out of college and early in my career, I worked in the group-sales department of The Registry Resort, which has since changed hands and is now a Waldorf Astoria. As a young professional, I was good at what I did. I could bury my nose in my computer and pump out proposals, contracts, and respond to sales inquiries with the best of them.

My two direct managers and the department manager recognized my skills and abilities. They appreciated and valued my assistance. But, beyond the walls of our shared office, very few knew my name, let alone my role in the organization.

I didn't realize how much I blended into the background until our corporate vice president of sales and marketing arrived for a quarterly visit. Although we had met on several occasions, he always "re-introduced" himself to me, as if I were a new employee, each time he arrived.

The first time this happened, I was terribly offended. How could he not know who I was? I was a great employee!

Then I stepped back and watched how he greeted the other sales team members. Some got the generic "It's so nice to meet you" handshake, while others got a much warmer greeting. He knew their names, their latest sales booking and something personal about them.

On that day, I decided I wanted to be noticed. I didn't know a thing about what a personal brand was, but I knew I wanted to get promoted, to be one of the decision makers, and, of course, make lots of money.

I started taking note of the people who were unsinkable, the ones who had dynamic personalities and attracted people. The people they attracted weren't just people who "needed" something, but people who could help these "unsinkables" achieve their goals. The unsinkable people routinely exceeded their sales numbers and seemed to have an easier time getting their work done. They were calm, cool, and enjoyed their jobs.

I knew that in order to achieve my goals, I would need to be more like them and get noticed.

What do you want out of Brand [You]?

It doesn't matter what level you have attained in your career or if you are starting a second career; it is much more difficult to achieve success.

Without a personal brand in place, you will struggle to succeed. That's true no matter what level you have reached in your career or if you are beginning a second career.

Have you ever had that awkward moment at a networking event in which a stranger asks you what you do and you are at a loss for words? You stumble through an explanation of where you work and then reply that you do sales, business development, or some other generic title.

In an attempt to understand you more effectively, the stranger asks the quintessential networking question, "Who is your ideal customer?" To which you respond, "Well, everyone loves widgets, so pretty much anyone."

Because that person you just met had to struggle to try to understand you, you left a negative impression.

Even worse, you didn't give the person a clear understanding of what you consider to be a solid contact or relationship. "IF" that person tries to be nice and send you a lead, it is more likely to be a friend's secretary's uncle who "really needs" your services, but probably has zero interest in paying for your services.

You've wasted your valuable time. Not just in attending a networking event, but you've wasted time talking to someone who still has no clue who you are, what you offer or why anyone should care.

To make matters worse, you can plan to waste some more time on the lousy leads that may come out of the encounter.

Working smart starts with having a clear perspective of who you are, where you are going and how you are going to get there.

In Building Brand [You], we are going to teach you how to take a good, hard look at where you are now. Only then can you evaluate your priorities and values to establish a clear vision of where you want to end up in life. I like to call that [You]topia, or, your ideal life.

When you take the time to set your goals, you are creating the right mindset of where you want to be. When someone asks you who you are or what you do, you will be prepared with a sharp and easy-to-understand answer. You will leave a lasting impression of what you offer – which is 1,000 times more important than what you do.

Additionally, when you have that clear direction in your life, you will start attracting more of the right kind of relationships in your life. It isn't about a "need" to be liked and popular. It is about being more comfortable in who you are so that people are comfortable around you. And when people are more comfortable with you, you won't have to chase down business because you'll get the right kinds of referrals in the first place.

With Brand [You] in place, you will not waste time at the wrong networking events or chasing unqualified leads. You will make more effective use of your time.

In my experience

Through the years, I've helped businesses and non-profits grow. As a small business owner, my own professional growth has validated the process that I am outlining.

My experiences at The Registry Resort confirmed that without a personal brand in place, I was a faceless part of the crowd. I worked hard just to be overlooked for promotions and passed over.

As I worked to build my brand in the community, I took the time to build solid relationships by aligning my brand with established and well-respected leaders.

It took more than a business card exchange to generate the trust and confidence that made my brand stick. It took a vibrant vision of where I wanted to go and the dedication to get there.

Today, many years later, I have established myself as a creative and results-oriented public relations professional who is tapped in to the community. I built solid relationships, generated profitable business opportunities and became a center of influence.

When I officially launched my business, I began updating my social media profiles and switched my job title and business name on LinkedIn. The next day, one of my first clients called me. He told me he saw my new business, he liked the work I had done and wanted to see if I could help him on some public relations projects.

A social media status update may have inspired a phone call, but it was my brand that led to a two-year contract with one the largest and most respected air-conditioning contractors in Southwest Florida, Conditioned Air.

Building Brand [You] will teach you exactly what you need to know to build your personal brand to take you where you want to go in life. You'll benefit from the lessons I learned the hard way and from examples of powerful brands we all know. You will learn what I learned by working with major brands and from the savvy mentors who have helped me develop my business.

When you have finished the book, you will be ready to build Brand [You].

7 LESSONS IN BUILDING BRAND [YOU]

1. You are Brand [You]

Some business professionals sacrifice a lot to climb to the very top of the corporate ladder, only to realize they don't like the view when they get there. If what you do in life doesn't leave you fulfilled, it will certainly leave you drained and eventually repel the most important people in your life.

Building Brand [You] isn't about living up to someone else's expectations of you or about setting safety nets for what you "might" want to have someday. It is about setting the direction in your own life so that you can confidently look at yourself in the mirror each morning, knowing that you are Brand [You].

2. Set your sights and your goals for [You]topia

Completing tasks may help you feel busy, but you won't find fulfillment in tasks. Worse, it takes your future out of your hands.

The foundation of Building Brand [You] starts with establishing your goals, values and priorities so that your brand will take you where you want to go. While many people recognize the value of setting goals, too few take the time to sit down and actually draft out goals that are in line with their values and priorities.

With a solid foundation in place, you can easily stay on track by doing something you love in a genuine and sincere manner. You won't have to "work" at your brand because it will be a natural extension of who you are. It will be easier to live out your dreams because you are exactly who you want to be.

In this section, we will explore your goals and define what I like to call [You]topia.

3. Value Brand [You] or no one else will

Many brands (personal and corporate) undercut their own value by reducing prices or offering cheap giveaways or gimmicky promotions. These short-term gimmicks may attract some attention, but it is usually the wrong attention. The next shiny new object that comes along will just as easily distract customers attracted by gimmicks. If you want to build long-term success, you need to assess your skills and accomplishments to understand the true value that you offer. Only then will others appreciate that value.

4. Build your network wisely

An evaluation of the commitments of one of my executive clients revealed that he was spending an average of 20 hours per week volunteering at the local chamber of commerce. That volunteer work equaled another part-time job on top of his full-time job and his six other networking groups. Dozens of volunteer hours generated fewer than 5 percent of his business leads. In building your network, we will set up a system to organize and prioritize your relationships so that you can build your network wisely.

5. Brand [You] must be simple, short and strong

In three seconds or less, people are sizing you up and asking themselves an important question: "Are you someone I need to know?"

With Brand [You] in place, you will change others' perspectives. Instead of wondering "if" you are worth investigating, you will leave them with a strong and compelling understanding of who you are. When they see you, they are going to ask "How do I get to know you?"

6. Smart Brands Speak Up

Fear keeps many people from sharing their accomplishments. At a base level, we are all a little afraid of the potential rejection or even looking like a jerk to friends. Putting yourself out there can certainly be a scary proposition. But the consequences of NOT sharing your story can be much greater.

When you choose to share who you are – both personally and professionally – you create the possibility of building a common, memorable connection with someone. These connections are about more than a mutual love of peanut butter; they are about finding a common ground of mutual trust that will enable you to work together toward a mutual interest like [You]topia.

Speaking up and expressing your brand enables you to build a strong relationship with people who understand the value of your brand and who will consistently refer the right kind of customers who will drive your growth.

7. Be relevant or be replaceable

The smartest brands are always growing and evolving to stay relevant. But how do you know what is working and what needs to be adjusted? In Building Brand [You], you will learn to construct a strong foundation of core values and goals. At the same time, you'll learn why you need to evolve over time to stay relevant.

Honest feedback from respected sources helps keep your messages focused. This reliable feedback helps you adjust how you express your brand and stay relevant in your profession and in your life.

The benefits of Building Brand [You]

Building Brand [You] will set the direction in your life by establishing goals and priorities that are meaningful to you.

You will live as the person you want to be and expressing that [You] authentically, intentionally, consistently and confidently, in every way possible.

With Brand [You] in place, you will spend more time focused on what is truly meaningful to you, such as advancing your career, enhancing your education, or spending more time with family and charitable ventures.

On the other hand, if you float through life without identifying your personal brand, you are placing your future in someone else's hands. It is like saying, "I want to watch the news," then giving the remote control to a five year old who is going to flip the channel over and over and over. Once in a while, she will hit a news station, but she will keep flipping.

If you are tired of living this way, it is time to build Brand [You] and take control of your life.

CHAPTER ONE

IT ALL BEGINS WITH A BRAND

"Brands are about creating emotional connections," Mickey Nall, APR, Fellow, managing director at Ogilvy Public Relations Worldwide.

Many people assume a brand is simply "a class of goods identified by name as the product of a single firm or manufacturer", as defined by the Merriam-Webster Dictionary. They confuse a brand with the legalities of a trademark, company and product names.

In this day and age, that definition may work for legal purposes, but it certainly won't help you develop the powerful brand recognition you need to succeed in your career.

Your brand is a summary of every customer's experience with you and his or her emotional reaction to that experience.

> Branding sets the direction and tone for the rest of your promotional efforts such as marketing, public relations and sales.

You have to begin with a brand. If you don't have a clear idea of your brand and the value it offers, you run the real risk that other people will shape your brand into something you don't want to be.

Branding sets the tone and direction for all promotional efforts from public relations to marketing and sales. It helps shape the message so that you stay consistent and true to the end goals on your path. It is the core essence of who you are, where you are going and how you are going to get there.

Once you set the right tone with your brand, it is much easier to chose the right tools to help you get to your end goal. With your brand in place, it will be much easier to manage your day-to-day relationship and marketing efforts to generate profitable results.

The common link behind the most sought after brands is trust.

Without trust, a brand has no value. This is true for both low-priced, generic, value brands and high-priced, luxury brands.

People with a particular need or desire seek out something to fulfill that desire. In a world full of plenty of options, a trusted brand is where people turn most of the time.

To establish trust in your customer's mind, you have to follow a strategic process to make your brand recognizable. This process is critical, not only for name recognition, but because it forces you to develop a solid understanding of what your brand offers to fulfill your customers' desire at the exact time they need you.

Your brand becomes more than a random encounter with some marks on a paper. In your customers' mind, your brand becomes a promise to fix their problems and serve as a reliable solution. Your brand promises exactly what they can expect to get from you, be it a morning cup of coffee, a prestigious BMW, or a trusted expert (you) to guide them.

As people grow and their needs change, their expectations from your brand will also evolve and change. Your brand must consistently deliver exactly what your customer needs, but it must be adaptive and responsive enough to respond to the changing desires of your customer base.

Brands that have been successful for a moment in time have built trust.

Successful brands that have stood the test of time have built targeted trust.

"A brand that captures your mind gains behavior. A brand that captures your heart gains commitment," Scott Talgo, principal and cofounder of Galea Consulting Group.

Lasting and powerful brands engender trust by taking the time to:

- Identify a core customer base.

- Understand customers' needs, hopes and desires.

- Create a valuable product or service that fulfills a specific need.

- Appeal specifically to the emotional needs of their core customer base and build trust.

Without a targeted customer base, you can build a brand that attracts the wrong type of customer for your product or service. Even worse, a poorly targeted brand may leave your core customers questioning if they can trust you and repel the people you need most.

Starbucks' mission to inspire and nurture the human spirit.

In 1971, the first Starbucks store opened. Inspired by Moby Dick, the name Starbucks was reminiscent of the high seas and early coffee traders. The store offered the "world's finest fresh-roasted whole bean coffees"(according to the company's website).

In the early 1980s, the company evolved with the new vision of its chairman, president and CEO, Howard Schultz. During a trip to Italy, Schultz was introduced to a more intimate coffee experience, one that brought people together to talk, share and build community.

Perhaps Schultz found his first customer by looking in a mirror. He was passionate about the pleasure of enjoying a fine cup of coffee and sought a way to enhance his customers' experience.

But, who would pay $4 for a cup of coffee they could make at home for pennies?

People who...

...need to get out of their daily routines to be inspired.

...care about treating others with dignity and respect.

...want to treat themselves to a personalized indulgence.

With the changing dynamic of the workplace and the demands of home life, people needed a third place to relax, unwind, and feel connected. They needed a place to be inspired without the pressures of their daily routines.

Building Trust:

If you walk into a Starbucks, you can trust that you are going to get a freshly brewed cup of coffee served by a friendly and knowledgeable barista. You may or may not care for the store, but it is reliable, and, when it is convenient, you may stop.

Building Targeted Trust:

Dedicated Starbucks fans find more than a "cup of Joe" during their regular coffee stops. They may go once a day or a couple of times a week, but what they find at Starbucks is more than any cup of coffee. They find inspiration.

From the moment they walk into a Starbucks store, they let their guard down and a comfortable feeling washes over them. It could be the plush couches, the modern decor with easily accessible laptop plugs, or the friendly barista who remembers how they like their coffee.

They may live in a world that isn't always fair, but they can sleep at night because when they buy that $4 cup of fair-trade coffee, they know that every person who touched that coffee was treated with dignity and respect, from the farmer to the processor to the barista, and, of course, themselves.

This corporate brand has left its mark by inspiring and nurturing the human spirit. Not because of a logo, but because of the experience its customers have from the moment they walk into each coffeehouse, to the second the last drop of coffee hits their lips.

> Like every brand, Starbucks has had its challenges, from negative corporate perceptions to poor customer service. The company has responded to customer feedback to stay true to its core mission: "to inspire and nurture the human spirit - one person, one cup and one neighborhood at a time."

In 2008, the company responded to complaints of poor customer service by shutting down for a day to retrain their baristas. While some called this a publicity stunt, a clear message was delivered to both employees and customers: Starbucks baristas will treat all customers and employees with dignity and respect.

Starbucks continues to flourish among its devotees because it has taken the time to understand what is important specifically to its target customers and taken the time to build the emotional connection that keeps them coming back. That mermaid on the side of the Starbucks cup represents so much more than "a class of goods." It is a promise that you will find a good cup of coffee and an inspirational experience.

How does Targeting and Trust translate to a personal brand?

As humans, we are always lumping and categorizing things into various little containers. Our brains are hardwired to do this so we can process and prioritize information that we need to know. Is it important or not? Funny or scary? Truthful or questionable?

On a surface level, you might see two very different products that share the same logo and know they are from the same manufacturer or brand name.

But, on a much more subtle level, you are assessing that brand.

- Does it look dated and old, like a stodgy, unkempt, government building?

- Or is it modern, minimalist and new, like an Apple store?

- Is there an app for that brand that allows you to digitally weave it into your high-tech lifestyle?

- Or, does the brand leave you enchanted and reminiscent of a romantic love story, like Romeo and Juliet?

- Does the brand make you feel confident you are buying something that will make your life easier and more productive?

- Or, does the brand make you cringe at the thought of spending endless hours on the phone with a poorly trained customer service representative before you can even use it?

In a split second, your subconscious mind is sizing up that brand to see if it is the right fit for you.

Going back to the Starbucks example, millions of people love ordering a "grande, double-shot, skinny caramel macchiato" and can't wait for the seasons to change so they can get pumpkin spice lattes and iced peppermint mochas.

Yet millions of others prefer to get coffee at a locally owned cafe that offers organic coffee and a choice of rice milk, almond milk, coconut milk or cow's milk. They want to feel as though they are supporting our earth and a local business.

Then, there are also millions of others who prefer to get coffee at a locally owned cafe like Food & Thought based in Naples, Florida. Founded by Frank Oakes, a long-time agribusiness entrepreneur, Food & Thought distinguishes itself with a brand of "militantly organic" in its grocery, cafe and retail store.

The store began with a small, but dedicated following of customers who sought the organic lifestyle. By delivering on their brand promise of providing healthy organic options, Food & Thought expanded its offerings and has attracted more and more health-conscious consumers. What started out as a hole-in-the-wall cafe next has more than quadrupled in size because it had a vision and took steps to build targeted trust among its health-conscious clientele.

Whether you are passionate about inspiring and nurturing the human spirit or prefer the health benefits of being militantly organic, you are a part of a target market for each of those businesses. Your preferred coffee shop offers something of specific value to you, something you trust you are going to get every time you pick up that latte.

When building Brand [You], you must work on building trust with the right targeted customer for you.

While some professionals have taken the simplest and most literal definition of a brand -- as a unique "thing" that identifies you -- they have forgotten or neglected to build the substance behind the brand.

For example, building your brand around a ladybug pin, a stylish hat, or a swanky address without understanding the ramifications is, at best, a silly gimmick. At worst, it could be repelling your ideal customer. And it certainly isn't a brand.

Perhaps in the Disneyland days of our economy, when money flowed freely, a gimmick could keep you top of mind. But when the tides change and money gets tighter, people are much more selective about what they buy and who they trust.

When it comes time to make an investment, who do you think has earned more trust? People who hang their hats on a gimmick?

Or the ones who have established a brand with substance to back it up?

The literal definition of a brand is a unique identifier. But, on a more complex level, a brand is a summary of every customer's experience with you and their emotional reaction to you.

What is the most important emotion people need to feel about you and your brand?

Trust.

Trust that you are going to provide exactly what they need or want, when they need or want it.

You will express your brand in many ways, from the clothes you wear to the way you answer your phone to the signature items you display.

And, yes, a ladybug might be an appropriate way to express your brand. If you are an expert in insects, gardens, plants or pollination patterns, being known as the ladybug lady would be appropriate. People will trust you to help their gardens grow.

But if you are a corporate banker in a male-dominated industry, being known as the Ladybug Lady won't earn you much trust.

In 2012, American Banker magazine recognized Scotiabank's Alberta G. Cefis as one of the 25 most-powerful women in banking. When asked about advice to provide females in the banking profession, Cefis responded:

> "For anyone striving to build a career in a competitive industry, I still recall the premise of Tom Peters who wrote, 'The brand called you'

in *Fast Company*. Peters said that individuals are as much a brand as Nike or Coke.

Thus, you should identify the qualities that make you distinctive from your colleagues. For women, we shouldn't have to emulate men, but instead build our own areas of differentiation.

I feel that my three points of differentiation are my abilities to: articulate a compelling vision and translate it into strategy, build high performing teams, and deliver through faultless execution."[1]

As an executive vice president and head of Global Transaction Banking, Cefis has built her brand as a leader around her ability to translate a vision into a strategic plan, then put the right people in the right places to make it happen.

She expresses her brand in a way that is meaningful and understandable to the executives in Scotiabank and peers in her industry, which has built trust and provided great opportunity for advancement.

Taking it to the next step, she continues to fortify her brand and trust by delivering on her brand promise. In the past year, Cefis is credited with expanding one of Scotiabank's business unit through global operations, as well as leading an initiative to improve cash-management technology.

YOUR NOTES

CHAPTER TWO

Breaking trust will break your brand

Years of work, strategy and influence can be lost in an instant when someone loses trust in Brand [You].

Your brand is more than an image on paper or a resume; it is a promise. It is an understanding that you will deliver on what people expect of you.

When a person truly trusts your brand, a lot has been invested in you. We're not just talking about a financial investment; we're talking about emotional investment.

When someone places trust in you, it becomes a very personal and emotional connection to your identity, even if you've never met the person. If you can't deliver on your brand promise, the consequences can be great.

Looking back even just a few years, it is easy to think of major brands that violated our trust in the most destructive ways.

The Deepwater Horizon Oil Spill

BP Oil Company

As an average American citizen, I bet your association with the BP brand never went much further than your experience at the local convenience store. If you needed gas on your way to work or a quick soccer game, you pulled into the local BP station to fuel up. It was clean and convenient, with reasonable prices and a friendly clerk. You've probably noticed BP advertising. Although you can't remember exactly what it said, it left you with a clean and happy feeling.

In your regular routine, you allowed BP into your life and trusted the "clean and happy" feeling you took away from your experiences there. Your perception of the brand was likely shaped by Connie the convenience clerk and your observations that BP was clean and easily accessible, not by any actual research into how the company operates.

The Government

The government rarely leaves people with a "clean and happy" feeling. Not a day that goes by that you don't hear the United States referred to as a "Regulation Nation". While many business owners are complaining about all the regulations that exist, you assume that means that the government is inspecting everything.

Meanwhile, the government doesn't advertise in the traditional sense, because that would look like spin. The government does community outreach projects to educate and inform citizens and businesses about their programs and how much they protect you.

Sometimes they say it directly and sometimes they imply it, but the government brand is built around protecting our people and our country from the Big Bad Wolf. The "wolf", in this instance, is everything from terrorists, to disease, to big businesses that want to hurt you.

Ironically, the government brand applies to all levels of city, county, state and national government, even though the branches of government operate relatively independently.

Because you rarely interact with the government, your perception of this brand relies on 30-second sound bites that appear on your news station. Again, you trust that brand is looking out for you based on little to no research of what they are actually doing.

Trust violated

On April 20, 2010, an explosion on the Deepwater Horizon killed eleven men and injured seventeen more, starting a chain of events that would wreak havoc for years to come.

BP was no longer clean and friendly.

Local BP convenience stores suffered from boycotts and vandalism as protestors raged against the company. It didn't matter that the local gas station was likely owned by a neighbor who had nothing to do with the corporate structure that was tied to the disaster.

The government was no longer protecting us from the big bad wolf.

Though some local city and state governments reacted swiftly with proper emergency management protocol, our trust in the government protecting us was shaken to extremes by the way local municipalities near the Gulf of Mexico handled the crisis.

As Americans, we were united in a state of grief, mourning and the harshest betrayal of trust you could fathom.

From a brand perspective, the public breach of trust occurred on April 20, 2010. However, for a crisis of this magnitude to have occurred, many years of ethical violations, corporate cultural issues and government mismanagement to place prior to this event.

The brand we thought we knew was only an artificial representation of what BP thought we wanted to see. It wasn't built on a true desire to be clean and friendly and the brand wasn't embraced throughout the corporate culture.

If the clean and friendly brand we thought we knew had been built on a solid strategic vision with core values and priorities, the circumstances of the Deep Water Horizon Spill would have been very different. While a tragic accident may have still occurred, the company's response would have been guided by a clear understanding of the corporate brand.

Hearts are broken every day

It is easy to look at these major crises and cry, "Corporate Brand FAIL!" But every day you are faced with choices that can confirm people have emotionally invested their trust in the right person (you) or that you are just another imitator who is going to let them down.

Have you ever had to run damage control after you clicked "Send" on an email that shouldn't have been sent?

When meeting with a client or a colleague, do you regularly arrive 15 minutes early or late?

If someone leaves you a message, can a response be expected from you within hours, days or weeks?

Have you jumped on a committee because you couldn't say no to a friend, then failed to meet any of your obligations?

Or, have you lost a client/job because you didn't keep your client or employer in the know about what you were doing?

We all have countless demands placed on us to be available and respond quickly. And, in the struggle to keep up, it is easy to trip and stumble.

You set the tone with your brand

Brand [You] does NOT have to live up to what other brands do. Brand [You] has to live up to the expectations you set in developing your brand.

If you need a fast lunch, waiting longer than five minutes at Chick-fil-A or McDonald's might leave you frustrated. But if you go to Shula's Steakhouse or Ruth's Chris Steakhouse, you could easily expect to wait an hour for the perfect steak.

Advertising on Groupon or LivingSocial requires the completion of an online application. Once you submit an application, you're told it will take two weeks to review and respond to your application. How would you react if you did not get that response and were hoping to have a quicker answer?

This is your chance to set the tone.

You can choose to offer luxurious, custom-designed dream homes or cookie-cutter tract homes.

You can choose to be quick, convenient and low-priced or an exclusive and expensive brand with long wait times.

When you build Brand [You], forget about catering to what you think people want because you'll just be setting yourself up for failure. As you craft your brand, make a promise to deliver consistently to ensure you maintain brand trust.

YOUR NOTES

CHAPTER THREE

1. YOU ARE BRAND [YOU]

"I am not looking like Armani today and somebody else tomorrow. I look like Ralph Lauren. And my goal is to constantly move in fashion and move in style without giving up what I am,"
Ralph Lauren, American fashion designer and business executive.

Building Brand [You] isn't about living up to someone else's expectations of you or about setting safety nets for what you "might" want to have someday. It is about setting the direction in your own life so that you can confidently look at yourself in the mirror each morning, knowing people are seeing you for exactly who you choose to be: the genuine and authentic Brand [You].

We all make mistakes in life, but if you are constantly reminding yourself that "I'm only human", you might just be giving yourself an excuse to fail. Whether you are accepting mediocrity or you are trying to meet other people's expectations, you are not fully committed to living your own life.

Building Brand [You] starts by establishing your goals, values and priorities so that your brand reflects the authentic you and a future that has your 100 percent commitment. Your career and lifestyle will leave you energized and ready to take on the next challenge.

Many of us have lived through difficult situations, from unemployment to medical setbacks to personal and professional losses. You can easily get caught up in the emotions and get "stuck" by allowing the situation define you rather than strengthen you.

By staying true to yourself, your brand will survive and even thrive following difficult times.

Leading after difficult times

As the Monica Lewinsky scandal unfolded in 1998, former First Lady Hillary Rodham Clinton had to go through one of our nation's most public politically charged sex scandals with her husband, President Bill Clinton. Coping with adultery is challenging enough for a "regular" person, but can you imagine dealing with personal issues in such a public forum?

The public humiliation would be enough to cripple most individuals. However, Hillary chose to stay in her marriage and continue to pursue her dreams.

In January 2001, she stepped into office with the newly earned title of U.S. Senator Hillary Rodham Clinton. She then set her sights on returning to the White House as the first female president, in 2008. Though her bid for the presidency was unsuccessful, she has continued to rise through the ranks of our government and was appointed the 67th U.S. Secretary of State in 2009. [2]

The Clinton family is still highly respected by many American people, despite the financial and adulterous scandals that would have emotionally crippled most individuals. Hillary Clinton had a dream of leadership that allowed her to hold strong through the most difficult of times.

Brand [You] Lesson: What doesn't kill you makes you stronger. Learn from the mistakes of the past. Let them go. Move on to bigger things.

Following your own path might be more difficult

Stefanie Joanne Angelina Germanotta was a musical prodigy who learned to play piano by age four. She was accepted to The Juilliard School at age eleven, but chose to go to a Catholic school instead. Her musical skills progressed as she wrote her first ballad at the age of thirteen and began performing live a year later.

Stefanie was one of only twenty students in the world to be granted early admission to the Tisch School of the Arts[3], only to withdraw a short time later to pursue her creative inspiration. A young prodigy with unlimited potential, she found herself working three jobs to make ends meet.

Years later, inspired by a passion for couture design and her love of music, Stefanie Joanne Angelina Germanotta became an international musical star more widely known as Lady Gaga, with an unmistakable brand as "Mother Monster" to millions of adoring fans. She also began the Born this Way Foundation to empower and inspire the next generation.

Extraordinary opportunities that appear before you aren't always the right opportunities. You have to follow your dreams and sometimes that means choosing the more difficult path in the short term, for much greater rewards.

Brand [You] Lesson: Sometimes choosing the right path for you might be more uncomfortable in the short-term. But when you are committed to your dreams, you can achieve anything.

Sometimes you have big shoes to fill

Once in a while the greatest opportunities come with even greater pressure to live up to the person who came before you. With confidence in your brand, your goals and your vision, you can easily take charge and lead with your style while staying true to company culture.

Thousands of books have been written about Steve Jobs' beloved leadership style and company. With a company brand so entrenched in the Jobs' way and millions of loyal fans who idolized him, Apple faced a real challenge (and potential crisis) in finding a successor who could lead the company into the future.

By all accounts, Tim Cook, CEO of Apple and successor to Steve Jobs' legacy, has successfully led the company through the challenge of Jobs' death and continued to innovate with "insanely great" technology.

In 2012, Cook was named one of *Time* magazine's 100 Most Influential People. His "Time 100" biography, written by Al Gore, describes Cook as "soft-spoken, genuinely humble and quietly intense"[4], the exact opposite of Jobs' personality.

If Cook had tried to emulate Jobs' personality to "fill the shoes" he had been left with, do you think the results would have been the same? Or do you think staff and consumers would have lost trust in Apple's brand and the future of products?

Cook succeeded because he genuinely believes in the Apple culture and he stayed true to himself, engendering trust from his staff, board and consumers.

Brand [You] Lesson: When you are committed to a vision--either as an individual or as a part of a larger corporate culture--you can stay true to yourself and build trust.

As you build your brand, you may have to wear multiple hats

Entrepreneurs such as Joe Pulizzi have a drive to succeed that often inspires them to start multiple business opportunities. Pulizzi is the founder of Z-Squared Media, SocialTract, Junta 42, and now focuses his efforts on the Content Marking Institute.

When I had the opportunity to speak to Pulizzi about his business ventures, I asked what he would change if he could go back to the beginning and start over. He said he wholeheartedly believed and cared about the businesses he started. Some were more successful than others, but he learned valuable lessons from all of them.

As he developed his brand, it all revolved around his passion for content marketing. Though the business model was tweaked with each of his companies, the passion remained the same and Pulizzi's brand identity as a content marketing expert thrived.

Unfortunately, some people undercut their own brands by fracturing who they are and what they do. Have you ever been introduced to someone who hands you a business card for their professional consulting business and then hands you a card for a jewelry business, or multi-level marketing product?

Worse yet, the professional consultant cards are home-printed on perforated business cards, while the multi-level marketing cards are professional-grade. What impression does that leave you about the person's commitment as a consultant? Or about their capabilities?

Brand [You] Lesson: When you are committed to following your passion, your business names may change and evolve, but the brand you are passionate about will stick with you.

Learn from Your Mistakes,
Choose Your Own Path,
Be True to Yourself,
Be Passionate,
Be [You]
— *Cyndee*

YOUR NOTES

CHAPTER FOUR

EXERCISE

GAIN PERSPECTIVE ON BRAND [YOU]

Sometimes, you get the best perspective from the outside looking in.

Take a lesson from Josh Miles, principal and founder of Miles Design. Miles has developed a unique niche providing high-end brand consulting to very technically oriented clients such as accountants, architects, engineers and software developers. While highly skilled in their industries, these technically oriented clients often have a difficult time translating their professional services into solid marketing messages.

When I asked Miles how he was able to help such technical and detail-oriented professionals work through the creative process, he said he starts by interviewing his clients' customers. During the interviews, he asks how his client is perceived. He's looking for the "stickiest marketing message" that can help give voice to his clients' brands.

This outside perspective helps give both Miles and his client an insight into what attracted the customer in the first place. Often, those insights are valuable messages about his clients' brand that were taken for granted or overlooked completely.

In one example, Miles described working with a well-established accountant. Once they started developing the brand voice, they uncovered the following brand statement: "It's not just about the numbers, it's about what they mean."

With his customers' insights, the accountant was finally able to express what he had been trying to say for more than twenty-five years.

Pick three to five of your best friends, customers, or colleagues and invite them out to lunch. Let them know you are revamping your brand and would value their honest opinions. Then ask them:

- What kind of image do I project?
    - Tell me more…
- What do you think I do best?
    - Tell me more…
- Who do you think my best customer is?
    - Tell me more…
- Is there anything that you think I need to work on?
    - Tell me more…

You will get the most value out of this feedback by sitting back, listening and taking notes. People often take a little while to warm up, so you may have to follow up with "Tell me more…" to get to the real answer.

Is this the [You] that you want to be?

_____
_____
_____
_____
_____

What is one positive characteristic you want to maintain / enhance?

_____
_____
_____
_____
_____

What is one negative characteristic you need to work on?

_____
_____
_____

_____

_____

Shape and refine [You] by setting your goals in the next chapter.

_____

_____

_____

_____

_____

YOUR NOTES

CHAPTER FIVE

2. SET YOUR SIGHTS AND YOUR GOALS FOR [YOU]TOPIA

"If you want to be happy, set a goal that commands your thoughts, liberates your energy and inspires your hopes."
Andrew Carnegie, self-made steel tycoon and philanthropist.

For years we've been taught to make our goals S.M.A.R.T. (Specific, Measurable, Attainable, Relevant, and Timely).

While the principles of S.M.A.R.T. goal setting are sound, they have left many professionals feeling stupid and spinning in circles because they lack vision and passion. Without a clear vision to focus on and the passion to keep us motivated, it is easy to dismiss a sensible and S.M.A.R.T. goal setting system.

Motivational speakers selling one goal-setting system or the next have hyped us up. For the average person, goal setting can be a painful process of fear and anxiety, followed by the disappointment and acceptance of yet another goal dropped.

Inevitably, December brings with it the pressure to set the perfect New Year's resolution, because next year will be your year to get "it" right. Unfortunately, four out of five of us won't accomplish our New Year's resolutions. And one in three won't even make it through January. It's not just "socially acceptable" to fail at these goals, it is trendy to flip the proverbial finger at them as they drop.

New Year's goal setting is just a scam anyway, right?

Why do you have trouble sitting down and setting your goals? Or, if you can get them written, why can't you seem to stick to them?

Clutter.

Plain and simple. There is too much clutter and not enough purpose in our day-to-day lives.

From a barrage of texts and tweets to your daily news sound bites, plenty of distractions could be put on hold with better time management. But I'm not just talking about "junk mail" clutter that can easily be cleared away.

Many of us are dealing with significant issues, from the demands of our career to family obligations, home repairs and health issues. So many things truly need to be done to get through today that all of the long-term, strategic planning gets pushed off until tomorrow. Only, as we all know, tomorrow ends up being much more than a day away.

How many times have you looked at that S.M.A.R.T. goal planning sheet and thought to yourself, "I'll think about that tomorrow... I know where I'm going anyway." Or, "I just need to get through this project. Then I'll have time to think about my goals."

In his book, "Think and Grow Rich", Napoleon Hill describes the common threads of the most successful businesspeople. Business icons like Henry Ford and Andrew Carnegie probably never started their days by filling out a neatly organized goal sheet in a three-ring binder. And I would guess they never did quarterly or annual life-goal progress reports.

This isn't to say they didn't have accountability in their lives or their businesses. I'm certain they did. Ford was known for his meticulous attention to detail.

But as Hill discusses, their ultimate goals were so much deeper than a goal written on a paper. These men built their business empires by starting with a dream and a clear vision of the businesses and lives they wanted to build.

Their dreams weren't just something that would be "nice" to do if they could get to it. Their dreams were rooted in a burning desire so intense that they had to pursue it. They thought of their dreams so intensely that it became a daily obsession. They spent every waking moment thinking about how to accomplish their goals.

Certainly there are those who turn their life goals into a negative obsession for wealth. Bernard Madoff bilked thousands of investors to the tune of $18 billion dollars. In 2001, Enron Executives bankrupted a company and stockholders with their pursuit of greed.

For every bad seed, there are a thousand that, when properly sown and nourished, can feed a nation.

Think about the accomplishments of Gandhi, who has been called the most influential man on earth. His goal, his life purpose, his obsession, was the pursuit of peace. In his time, he influenced millions of followers to follow his vision with peace - without worrying about being S.M.A.R.T. about his goals.

What about Steve Jobs and the "Apple Nation"? From the depths of his garage, he had a vision of a computer that was more than a computer. He had a clear vision of a personal-computer revolution that built a cult-like following of admirers and customers.

In 2012, an Austrian man lived out his boyhood dream by breaking records and the sound barrier. As a child, Felix Baumgartner saw his dream clearly. He was going to break Joe Kittinger's 1960 record for longest skydive from more than nineteen miles. In a partnership with Red Bull, Felix took on the mission to the edge of space and successfully lived out his obsession, completing a twenty-four-mile-high freefall from the earth's stratosphere.

Would you call each of these people successful?

Though the book "Think and Grow Rich" was written in 1937, the fundamental principles still apply to the most successful individuals of our generation. Despite their wildly different brands and their completely different achievements, each of these men started with a clear vision of what they wanted out of life.

"If you aim at nothing, you'll hit it every time," Unknown.

THE FIRST STEP IN BUILDING BRAND [YOU] IS TO DEVELOP A VISION OF YOUR [YOU]TOPIA

Originally conceived by Sir Thomas More in 1516, Utopia was an imaginary country where everyone lived in peace and harmony under ideal conditions. Though the country doesn't exist, the pursuit of happiness still propels people to this internal place of peace and ideal perfection.

> **[You]topia is a clear vision of your ideal life.** It is the place where your career ambitions intersect with and complement your personal desires. It is where your base-level needs for food and shelter are easily met and you seek self-actualization. It is where you are most confident and comfortable about who you are and what you have to offer. It is where you wake up in the morning with a sense of purpose, determination and direction. It is both a legacy that you want to leave and an ideal state of mind to be living in and enjoying right now.

> *Great leaders know that they must ultimately answer to the vision they have set. The vision is the beacon toward which they lead their team. Even when morale is down, detractors are everywhere, great leaders always answer to the vision. Every great innovation that has ever happened first started with a vision and ultimately came to reality because of a staunch commitment to that vision.*
>
> Mike Michalowicz, CEO of Provendus Group[6]

[You]topia must be your vision

The 1998 drama-comedy, "The Truman Show", featured Jim Carrey (starring as Truman) living in the Utopian town of Seahaven. Unbeknownst to him, Truman's near-perfect life is built around an artificial movie set that begins to crumble around him. As the picture-perfect set shatters, his desire for true love takes over.

In the end, Truman breaks out of his artificially constructed version of perfection: the set he used to call home. He takes control of his future and chooses to live his own life. And, in true Hollywood style, he gets the girl, too!

We can learn two very important lessons from "The Truman Show":

1) Truman's life was an artificial reality, scripted by other people, using their ideas of what makes a perfect life. If you are living in someone else's vision of a perfect life, eventually that reality will come crumbling down around you.

2) When Truman finally realized what he wanted (the woman he fell in love with), he had to face his fears and go to extreme lengths to break free from his former life. It was extremely difficult and a whole town turned against him. But he relentlessly pursued his dream and got the girl.

Once you have figured out what your [You]topia is, you have to be willing to do whatever it takes to get there.

Getting started on [You]topia

As I described with Gandhi, Jobs, and Baumgartner, success can be achieved in wildly different ways. The same holds true with [You]topia. The only vision of an ideal state of [You]topia is your version.

Before you take a step forward, let's take half-step back. Remember why people fail to achieve their goals?

Clutter.

How do you cut the clutter?

When was the last time that you attended a conference or weekend retreat? Maybe it was for work or a motivational retreat. Remember how peaceful you felt and how easily ideas flowed through you?

As you sat in the motivational keynote sessions, diligently taking notes and surrounded by people who were just like you, it was easy to step outside of your own head and clearly see the great answers for which you had been searching. You felt connected to people and life because you realized you were not alone.

The coffee served at those retreats has no magic power (unless it is laced with Red Bull?). And the three-ring binder filled with PowerPoint presentations, worksheets and inspirational quotes isn't what's special about the experience.

The magic lies in getting away from your day-to-day routine. When you attend those conferences, you purposefully take the time to focus on what is important to you and where you want to go. You cut through the clutter!

Imagine all of the money you could save, if you could just do that retreat in your own backyard!

Unfortunately, many of those breakout session breakthroughs often meet the same fate as New Year's resolutions. Another well-intentioned goal gets pushed aside as you wade through emails and catch up on your in-box.

Before you set out to contemplate what [You]topia is, set yourself up for success in this crucial step.

1) Set aside at least two hours. Studies show that it takes thirty minutes to get into focus on an issue. This one is too big for a fifteen-minute cup of coffee, so give yourself at least two hours. If you are an entrepreneur, schedule an official board retreat with yourself to process [You]topia.

2) Get out of your office or your house. Tons of things need to get done, but the first priority is setting up your vision for the future. Don't let the clutter of daily tasks creep in and collapse your future. If the budget for your official board retreat won't allow for a room at The Ritz-Carlton (although you are definitely worth it), then take an afternoon at the beach, on a boat or in a park. One of my favorite think spots is the coffee bar at Whole Foods. Maybe there is something magic in the coffee after all!

Right now, I'm writing from the comfort and convenience of my own backyard with about a dozen ginormous squirrels playing field hockey with peanuts and traipsing through the palm trees, sounding like a herd of elephants. Quiet? No. Does it make me laugh and make it easier to write? Yes.

3) Shake off what everyone else says. We are going to work on [You]topia, not [EveryoneElse]topia. This is about creating an ideal vision of your life, the way you want to live it. Of course, [You]topia will incorporate the most important people in your life, but at a fundamental level it is about putting the pieces together in the right way to create your burning desire. We aren't just setting a goal that can easily be forgotten; this is going to be your legacy or life's purpose. It should be so ingrained in your future that you can't forget it. You won't need to schedule quarterly "goal reviews" because you will live and breathe your [You]topia each and every day.

4) Get over the excuses for why you can't do something. It is so easy to think of reasons why you can't live out your wildest dreams. Once you come up with one reason why it won't work, new reasons will snowball. You can always tell yourself you don't have enough time, education, money, etc.

What you really need is one reason TO do it. At the center of it all is one reason that takes your [You]topia from "nice to do" to "need to do".

My reason for pursuing my [You]topia is simple. Her name is Bridget and she was born on Aug. 18, 2006. I often call her Mini-Me because she is a reflection of who I am and who I hope to be at the same time. Every morning, I want her to leave the house inspired to pursue her dreams, whatever they may be.

When life gets hard, I can look at her and remember why I am doing exactly what I NEED to be doing right this minute.

"Don't say you don't have enough time. You have exactly the same number of hours per day that were given to Helen Keller, Pasteur, Michelangelo, Mother Teresa, Leonardo da Vinci, Thomas Jefferson, and Albert Einstein," H. Jackson Brown, Jr., author of Life's Little Instruction Book.

WORKSHEET [YOU]TOPIA

"Everyone has limits – not everyone accepts them," Felix Baumgartner, Austrian skydiver and BASE jumper.

A million reasons exist to keep you from doing something. What is the one reason you have to make this [You]topia your reality?

_____

_____

_____

Visualize your life in ten years.

Forget about what you know you can do and focus in on what inspires you.

What would you dare to do if you knew you could not fail?

Would you start the business you've been dreaming of for years? One that revolutionizes the way we…(insert your inspiration here).

Would you jump from the edge of space like Felix Baumgartner?

Would you give up everything you own and dedicate your life to a greater good?

_____

_____

_____

_____

_____

Describe what you see, hear, and feel in your [You]topia.

What type of house do you live in?

Is it a mansion on the beach with an outdoor kitchen and pool bar fit for any party?

Is it a ranch-style home, with chocolate chip cookies baking in the oven?

Or is it a modern and minimalist condominium in the city?

Do you have a huge yard full of kids? Or dogs? Or perfectly manicured topiary trees?

Are you eating a home-cooked breakfast of bacon and eggs in your kitchen? Or sipping a mimosa and eating fresh strawberries and chocolate-laced croissants on your balcony at The Ritz-Carlton?

Who are the most important people there with you?

What do you enjoy doing together?

How do you spend your time?

Are you leading a business? Coming up with big ideas? Closing the sale?

Are you helping small businesses? Or working for a large corporation?

What is your title? Are you a C-suite executive (CEO, CFO, CMO)? Are you the owner of your own business?

Are you in flip-flops working on a laptop in your backyard? Or do you get up in the morning to put on your Gucci suit before your car service drives you downtown to your corner office on 5th Avenue?

Where do you spend your time when you aren't working? Are you surrounded by family? Saving an endangered species? Or seeking adventure around the next corner?

What does the word "family" mean to you? It could be as simple as a spouse, or perhaps "family" means having enough kids for a whole football team. You decide.

_____

_____

_____

_____

How do all of these questions help build your brand?

Picture Donald Trump. Where does he live? You don't know him personally, but can you guess if he is wearing flip-flops in the backyard or the latest designer suit in a corner office?

Now think of Oprah Winfrey, another extremely powerful executive. How does her house differ from Donald Trump's? After work, is she going to offer you a Scotch on the rocks or a Chardonnay?

The most powerful brands are not built around a logo or a design theme. The most powerful brands are a part of who you are, down to the very core of your being. Your brand is a reflection of every experience a person expects of you, through all five senses.

If you were to sit down with Trump to discuss business, it would be promptly scheduled into a 15-minute appointment at Trump Tower on Fifth Avenue in New York City. As you walk into an impeccably appointed executive boardroom, you would notice high-backed leather chairs and the latest electronic video conferencing equipment available at the push of a button. During your pitch, you'd better be prepared with key bullet points and the facts to back it up or you can expect to hear the famous words "You're Fired!"

But if you had a chance to talk to Oprah, you might expect to receive a glass of wine in some elegantly simple glasses. Because she is so approachable, your conversation could be drawn out for hours as you discuss the possibilities while lounging in a bright, airy living room on a plush, oversized sofa with an equally plush throw-blanket. The room would be lightly scented with some comforting floral fragrance.

By establishing a clear vision and expectation of what [You]topia -- your ideal life -- looks like, you are setting a fundamental foundation for what your brand is and what people will expect from you. Even better, this vision will be more meaningful and important to you; so instead of being one of the four out of five Americans who can't keep momentum on their goals, you will be the one who makes it.

Take your time to be detailed as possible in describing [You]topia. The more vividly you can see it, smell it, and hear it, the more you will continue to actively pursue it.

_____

_____

_____

_____

_____

_____

_____

_____

_____

_____

_____

_____

_____

_____

_____

_____

_____

YOUR NOTES

CHAPTER SIX

ALIGNING YOUR PRIORITIES WITH [YOU]TOPIA

It is one thing to set priorities; it is quite another to honestly live them. Now that you have a clear vision of [You]topia, it is time to clarify your priorities so that you can confidently spend your time on the most important people, activities and things that will help you stay energized and on track to [You]topia.

Many people would claim their priority list looks something like this:

1. Family

2. Work

3. Friends/Hobbies

However, when you add up where they are spending their time, you see a much different picture.

1. Spending 80 hours a week at work

2. Decompressing by spending a day with friends or hobbies

3. Lastly, the occasional dinner and homework time with the family

In this new world of blended families, working from home and smart phones that keep you connected to the office at all hours, it is easy to be physically present while letting your focus shift thousands of other places. As a mother and a business owner, I've found myself working through vacations and getting out just one more email to the exasperation of my family.

"Action expresses priorities," Mahatma Gandhi.

It is easy to justify the lapse in time because you need work to provide a house, food, and clothing for your family. And you need some time for your sanity so that you can enjoy the time with your family, right?

But this kind of misguided thinking often leads to burnout and regrets about the ways you "should" have been spending your time. Worse yet, it could lead to resentment of your life and cause serious damage to the relationships that mean the most to you.

Before you set your priorities, it is important to realize they must be YOUR priorities. This "Family - Work - Friends & Hobbies" model is missing several things, like: health, spirituality, education, or activism and giving back.

To feel the right life balance in Brand [You], your priorities should include:

- Health - If you are sick or in pain, how can you focus in on your goals or take a moment to let go and laugh out loud? Your health must be a key priority every day.

- Personal - This might be in the form of spirituality, working out, reading a book, or watching a sunset. You need some time to decompress from life and clear the clutter so that you can be in the moment when you are with your family or at work.

- Career / Job - We all have expenses to pay, so your career will help you acquire wealth to get there (whether it is a mansion on the beach, a cabin in the woods, or a studio apartment in an urban oasis).

- Family - The definition of family is constantly changing. It doesn't have to mean a spouse, two children and a dog. It can be your best friend, roommate, or a single-parent home. Maintaining a relationship with your family is important to keep you grounded.

- Education - When we stop learning, we stop growing. It doesn't matter if you want to learn how to grow a garden or to be a better salesperson, it is important to continue feeding your mind and growing.

- Hobbies or Fun - Think of something that inspires you, something that can get you out of your day-to-day routine and make you laugh.

- Activism and Giving Back - Volunteering helps us connect to a greater good through service to others. Perhaps this is through serving meals at a soup kitchen or lobbying to change an unjust law. You can leave your mark by taking a stand and taking action.

In an article written for the Harvard Business Review entitled, "If You Don't Prioritize Your Life, Someone Else Will", Greg McKeown describes that watching your language can also help focus on the right priorities.

> Every time we say, "I *have* to take this call" or "I *have* to send this piece of work off" or "I *have* to go to this client

meeting," we are assuming that previous commitments are nonnegotiable. Every time you use the phrase "I have to" over the next week, stop and replace it with "I choose to." It can feel a little odd at first — and in some cases it can even be gut-wrenching (if we are choosing the wrong priority). But ultimately, using this language reminds us that we are making choices, which enables us to make a *different* choice.[7]

As you transition through this process, your priorities might change. Perhaps it is more important to focus in on your education so you can change careers. Or perhaps you have been working too hard and now is a time you should be focused on having fun.

Take a minute to list the top five priorities in your life, in order of importance (1 being most important):

1._____

2._____

3._____

4._____

5._____

Creating this list may leave you feeling happy and content about the most important people and things in your life. But to truly align your priorities with [You]topia, we need to assess how you are spending your time and decide if your focus is on the priorities that are most important to you.

Below are twenty-four rectangles, representing the hours in the day. We all get the same amount of time in a day, but as you pursue Brand [You], you are going to be more strategic and thoughtful about where you spend your time.

Get out seven colored markers or use your pen to make different patterns in the rectangles below.

> 1. Take a pen or black marker and color in the number of hours of sleep you get in a day. This is necessary time, but it is also six to eight hours you are not spending on your priorities.

> 2. Choose another colored pen or marker to color in the number of hours you spend on daily routines, such as getting ready for work, commuting, etc. Again, this is part of what you have to do, but it doesn't relate to one of your priorities.

> 3. Then, with another color, mark off the time you spend working. Remember to include time in the office, networking and at special events (on average).

> 4. Next, mark off the time you spend on yourself. This could include exercising, reading a book, getting a spa treatment or unspecified personal time.

> 5. With another color, mark off the time you spend with family.

> 6. With another color, mark off the time you spend taking care of your health.

> 7. Fill in the remaining time with your other priorities.

Compare the hours in your day to your priorities. How many hours does your No. 1 priority get?

One of my executive clients completed this process and was visibly shaken. A dedicated father, his family was undoubtedly his No. 1 priority. But at the end of the day, he realized that he was spending an average of thirty minutes a day with his kids.

His actions were not aligned with his priorities and he was missing out on the thing that made him happiest in life. While we couldn't eliminate his job, he chose to be more selective about his time at business events so he could spend more quality time with his wife and children.

It isn't just a lack of family time that leaves people unfulfilled, though. Many women find themselves too heavily focused in on their families and regret that they downplayed pursuing education, career, or even taking care of themselves.

Now, the next step is to take another look at your day and how you would like to spend your time. Start by filling in the number of hours you would like to spend on each of your top five priorities. Then fill in work, sleep, and daily routines.

In comparing your average day to your ideal day, it should be apparent that something has to change.

You don't really need all that sleep, right?

Identify some of your time wasters, things you don't really care about and don't really need to do. Perhaps this includes reducing the amount of time getting ready in the morning so that you can start the day with a fifteen-minute yoga stretch. Or, perhaps you need to look for a way to live closer to work so you can reduce your commute time.

Now identify some meaningful ways to add in your priorities. Maybe you can't eliminate your commute time, but you could listen to an audio book as a way of fitting in some education. Can you approach your boss about using a flextime schedule, in which you work a couple of longer days so that you can coach sports two nights a week?

Maybe you can't take half-day off to volunteer in your child's classroom every week, but perhaps you could read a book and review homework with him or her every night?

Be cautious about multitasking though. Taking a walk with your spouse can be a pleasant way to help you prioritize both health and quality time with your family. However, if you want to take a walk to clear your head and you're too distracted to carry on a meaningful conversation with your spouse, you'll end up wasting the time and aggravating yourself and your spouse by taking the walk together.

Spell out the three changes you are going to make right now to start putting your true priorities first every day:

1._____

2._____

3._____

YOUR NOTES

CHAPTER SEVEN

WHAT ARE YOUR VALUES?

Personal values are core standards you set for yourself to direct your day-to-day life. Your values will shape your decisions on moral, ethical and everyday decisions. While personal values are shaped by family, religion and life experiences, they are highly personalized and can include many things.

Though you have a value system you live by, you likely aren't conscious of how often your values are guiding you to make daily decisions. On a subconscious level, your values are shaping your ambitions, dreams, and drive for success.

If you are living a life that is not in alignment with your values, you are more likely to feel uncomfortable and stuck in a bad situation. If your career takes you on a path that doesn't match your value system, it can lead to unhappiness and resentment that will tarnish your brand, hurt your career and boil over into your personal life.

On the flip side, when your career, family life and hobbies are in alignment with your value system, you are more likely to feel content and satisfied. Because you are focusing your efforts on what is most important to you, you will see the day differently. Instead of dreading all the things that you "have" to do, you will look forward to all of the things you "choose" to do.

And, when you are truly living your values, you will be able to form deeper relationships with customers, family, and friends, based on shared values. Your path to [You]topia will become more clear and the people who can help you achieve that vision will start appearing in your life.

Ben & Jerry's Ice Cream was founded by two men who loved dessert and wanted to improve the quality of life locally, nationally and internationally. Founder Ben Cohen merged his obsession for dessert with his obsession for peace, an obsession that is expressed on every pint of ice cream produced by the company.

> *"If you can form a relationship with your customers based on shared values, that is the strongest possible bond you can form,"* Cohen described. *"But finding shared values means you have to have some values, they can't just be milquetoast, namby-pamby middle-of-the-road crap. You need to stand for something, so customers who believe the same thing can glom onto your brand."*[8]

Starbucks Coffee values dignity and respect for all customers, employees, vendors and farmers. They express their values through the products they sell, the level of customer service they provide, and by being good neighbors in the communities that they serve.

As the global leader in beverage products, Coca-Cola and all of its affiliated brands value leadership and "The courage to shape a better future".

> In its 2011-2012 Global Sustainability Report, Chief Sustainability Officer Bea Perez described, "Coca-Cola is intent on growing our business by making a difference wherever our business touches the world and the world touches our business. We are committed to enhancing

people's lives, economically empowering women, providing access to safe water and promoting water replenishment - in collaboration with critical partners from civil society and government."

(Taken from Coca-Cola press room)

How do your values shape your brand?

By consciously identifying and prioritizing your values, you can make smarter decisions about a career path that will get you to [You]topia while having a lot more fun along the way. Living out your values in the most sincere and intentional way, you will also connect with people who share your values. As Cohen described above, these connections are stronger because of your shared values.

If you love your iPhone, iPad, or Mac you probably share Apple's values of simplicity and excellence.

If you know someone in the military, you can understand the values that Marines express with "Semper Fidelis" (always faithful).

Or the life of a military family, as my sister describes, "Semper Gumby" (always flexible).

> "At Zappos, our belief is that if you get the culture right, most of the other stuff -- like great customer service, or building a great long-term brand, or passionate employees and customers -- will happen naturally on its own. Your culture is your brand," Tony Hsieh, chief executive officer, Zappos.com. [9]

Zappos.com Culture was built around 10 Core Values

1. Deliver WOW through Service
2. Embrace and Drive Change
3. Create Fun and a Little Weirdness
4. Be Adventurous, Creative, and Open-Minded
5. Pursue Growth and Learning
6. Build Open and Honest Relationships with Communication
7. Build a Positive Team and Family Spirit
8. Do More with Less
9. Be Passionate and Determined
10. Be Humble

For Brand [You], understanding and identifying a strong set of values will help you make smart decisions to answer important questions, such as:

- What career is best for you?

- Should you accept a promotion to another city?

- Should you start your own business?

- Should you compromise with your boss or stand up for something you want to correct?

Defining your core values

Defining and understanding your core values can be a challenging task, but it is an important exercise. Your values are a central part of Brand [You] and where you want to go in life.

As you think about the questions below, consider times in your personal life and your career, because your values shape your entire life;

- Describe a time in your life when you were the happiest.
    - What were you doing?
    - Who was with you?
    - What was it about this moment that made you happy?
- Describe a point in time when you were proudest of your accomplishment.
    - What did you accomplish?
    - Why did this make you proud?
    - If others were present, why were they proud of you?
- Describe a time when you felt fulfilled and content with your life.
    - What were you doing?
    - How did this feel meaningful?

- **Circle all of the values below that you would like to be known for:**

Abundance	Determination	Growth
Accessibility	Dignity	Happiness
Accuracy	Diligence	Hard Work
Achievement	Discipline	Health
Adventure	Discretion	Helping
Altruism	Diversity	Honesty
Ambition	Duty	Honor
Assertiveness	Effectiveness	Humility
Balance	Efficiency	Independence
Beauty	Elegance	Ingenuity
Being the Best	Empathy	Inner Harmony
Belonging	Energy	Inquisitiveness
Benevolence	Enjoyment	Insightfulness
Boldness	Entertainment	Intelligence
Carefulness	Enthusiasm	Intuition
Celebrity	Excellence	Justice
Challenge	Excitement	Leadership
Cheerfulness	Expertise	Leaving a Mark
Cleanliness	Exploration	Legacy
Commitment	Expressiveness	Love
Community	Extravagance	Loyalty
Compassion	Fairness	Mastery
Competitiveness	Faith	Modesty
Conformity	Family	Motivation
Consistency	Fidelity	Neatness
Contentment	Financial Security	Obedience
Control	Fitness	Openness
Cooperation	Fluency	Originality
Courtesy	Focus	Passion
Creativity	Freedom	Patriotism
Curiosity	Fun	Peace
Decisiveness	Generosity	Perfection
Dependability	Grace	Piety

Positivity	Service	Timeliness
Practicality	Shrewdness	Tolerance
Precision	Simplicity	Tradition
Preparedness	Soundness	Trustworthiness
Professionalism	Speed	Truth
Reliability	Spontaneity	Understanding
Religion	Stability	Uniqueness
Resourcefulness	Strategic	Unity
Restraint	Strength	Usefulness
Results	Structure	Variety
Security	Success	Vision
Self-Actualization	Support	Wealth
Self-Control	Teamwork	Winning
Selflessness	Temperance	
Self-Reliance	Thankfulness	
Sensitivity	Thoroughness	
Serenity	Thoughtfulness	

Don't get caught up in other people's definitions of these values. For example, a lot of people think of "family" as a need to get married, have children and settle down. As a single parent and the daughter of divorced parents, the meaning of family at my home is a much broader version.

Narrow the list down to your top ten. If you arrive at two similar values, such as "wealth" and "abundance", choose the one that is more meaningful for you in your life and place an "X" or line through the other one.

Now, let's narrow the list even further. If you could only live by five of these values, which ones would you eliminate? Place an "X" through those.

The five remaining are your core values. Write them below:

1._____

2._____

3._____

4._____

5._____

Do these values match with the times in which you were the happiest? Proudest? Most fulfilled?

Do these values align with your priorities?

Do these values align with your vision of [You]topia?

Completing this process so that it is an accurate reflection of you is a critical foundation for building Brand [You]. It is Okay if you need to make adjustments through this process. Taking a little more time now is better than continuing to live with an unplanned and unfocused brand that leaves you spiraling and unsatisfied for years to come.

Once you are confident with your answers, move on and set your goals to reach [You]topia.

YOUR NOTES

CHAPTER EIGHT

SET YOUR GOALS TO ACHIEVE YOUR [YOU]TOPIA

"What you get by achieving your goals is not as important as what you become by achieving your goals."
Henry David Thoreau, American author and philosopher.

Getting from where you are now to your end vision of [You]topia may seem like an impossible journey. But, in the words of banker and philanthropist, J.P. Morgan, "The first step towards getting somewhere is to decide that you are not going to stay where you are."

The difference between wishing for a better life and making a better life is setting your plan to get there. Setting the right goals will help kick-start you into action and show you the incremental successes along the way that will keep you motivated when life gets in the way.

By taking the time to develop a strong vision of the life you want, a specific reason to stay on track, as well as the priorities and values you want to hold true to, we have given you direction and purpose for your goals. These goals will become part of your life because they will get you to [You]topia.

In building Brand [You], include both career and personal goals

Decades ago, work and home lives were separated into neat little compartments. When you went to the office, you had your water-cooler friends and people with whom you worked closely. Then you would go home to your family, neighbors, and Little League coaching.

Culturally, we have sought more work-life balance by blending these two worlds. Now, you may telecommute and only see your co-workers through Skype or Facebook. And, with the rise of social media, we experience an ever-shrinking sense of private family time as birthday, holiday and tailgating photos are emailed and posted online.

Remember how we defined a brand as "a summary of every customer's experience with you and their emotional reaction to you"? Before people can connect with you and to truly understand what you offer, you have to give them a personal connection to understand. Perhaps that is a shared value (competition), a shared priority (getting a child through college), or a shared vision of [You]topia (seeking out adventure around every corner).

Personal connections through these shared experiences are 1,000 times stronger than trying to break the ice through a cold call or a business-card exchange.

So, yes, include your personal goals!

> *"People are not lazy. They simply have impotent goals - that is, goals that do not inspire them," Tony Robbins, author and motivational speaker.*

Get emotionally involved with your goals

We started this section of the book questioning how far your S.M.A.R.T. goals had taken you. Though there are some variations, S.M.A.R.T. typically stands for Specific, Measurable, Attainable, Relevant, and Timely.

All of these principles are important considerations to include as you draft out your goals. Where SMART Goals fall short is failing to give meaning, purpose and a strong vision to your goals. By defining and understanding your [You]topia priorities and values, we have given you the very reason to stay true to your path and accomplish your goals while avoiding the distraction of other people's goals.

"Nothing changes until the pain of staying the same is greater than the pain of changing," Unknown.

Identify the most important goals to focus on right now

Have you ever wanted to drop five or ten pounds? Many people do and they frequently fail. One of my clients was carrying around a few extra pounds that left her very self-conscious in her suits and routinely low on energy.

She knew that to lose the weight, she would have to make a better effort to plan out healthy meals and make time for exercise. When I asked her why she didn't make the time, she claimed that she was too busy with this project or that project to take the time to prepare healthy meals. Basically, she had to take care of too many other people, but didn't prioritize taking care of herself.

What it all boiled down to was that, while the extra weight was uncomfortable, it wasn't causing her enough pain at the moment to spark her to make the change. She had more pain points or personal issues to deal with in the short term.

After seeing several people's lives turned upside down because of a serious illness, I personally believe that your health is the keystone to achieving the rest of your goals. If you don't have enough energy to get through the day, how are you going to have enough motivation to complete the next project at work? How can you truly laugh and lose yourself in the moment with your family and friends? How can you lose yourself in a good book if your back is hurting?

But health doesn't necessarily mean losing an extra ten pounds. Maybe your mental health comes from taking time to laugh with friends more often or getting an extra thirty minutes of sleep so that you have more energy during the day.

Regardless, your time and focus are limited. Choose the goal that is most important to you right now.

Keep your language positive and focused on how you can achieve your goals

Getting ahead in life is often a slight shift in perspective. Instead of focusing your thoughts on the issue in front of you, you have to train your brain to get around the issue that is blocking you to get what you are looking for. Just figure out how to take the next logical step.

I was trying to help a woman get through a difficult transition when she divorced her husband, who also happened to be a business partner. Her estranged husband wasn't making payments on a lease they had both signed and it was holding up her plans for her next business venture. She needed to contact the property manager to end the lease, but lacked some information. She was left stuck and feeling hopeless because all she could think was "I don't have the information that I need…".

I simply asked her, "Okay, how do you get that information?"

A short Google search later, we had exactly what she needed to resolve the situation.

While there may be several steps into your career before you get to your [You]topian lifestyle, you must think of each of your goals with the perspective of "How do I get to the next step?".

"The greater danger for most of us is not that our aim is too high and we miss it, but that it is too low and we hit it," Michelangelo.

Aim High!

Abandoned at birth by an unwed mother, Oprah Winfrey lived through years of abuse as she was bounced among foster homes and adoptions. She was raped at the age of nine, became pregnant at the age of fourteen, and abused drugs along the way. After rising above her early challenges, she began a career in television, where she was once fired because she was "unfit for TV".

Given her past, it would be easy to discard her goals and aspirations as unrealistic fantasies. Despite a less-than-humble upbringing, Winfrey pursued her dreams and has become one of the world's richest people.

"I feel that luck is preparation meeting opportunity," Oprah Winfrey, media mogul.

Many of the most successful individuals are driven to succeed because they have come from the most desperate and poverty stricken situations. If they set their minds on achieving what was "realistic", they might still be living in the slums and scraping by, paycheck to paycheck.

When you have a dream and a strong vision of your [You]topia, don't be afraid to set big goals to get there.

Pace yourself and prioritize your goals

Let's say your vision of [You]topia includes owning your own business as a cupcake maker. You need $10,000 to start up your dream business, but you also have a family to take care of, bills to pay and excessive debt from a few difficult years.

One of your other goals is to "eliminate your debt".

Can you eliminate your debt by adding another $10,000 to start your business?

These two goals are at odds with each other. You have to pick which one is more important right now and which one can be paced out over a longer term.

When the recession hit in 2007, I saw several businesses pop up. Many of the new business owners had worked in the real estate or construction industries and had lost their jobs. They mortgaged their homes and extended their credit on expensive business opportunities, risking their families' livelihood.

Unfortunately, these businesses were poorly planned and executed, leaving families in much worse situations than they would have been if they had never started a business.

However, a few of the businesses who started with smaller capital investments and ran on very tight budgets grew and flourished.

If two of your goals are "reduce debt" and "start a new business", prioritize which one is more important in the short term. You can achieve both, but you will likely have to incur some debt to start the new business, so you have to pick which one you will work on first.

Prioritize your goals so you achieve the most important first step. Set a mix of short-term and long-term goals so that you can see incremental progress, but keep looking down the road toward [You]topia.

Write down your goals.

According to Tom Hopkins, you are 1,000 times more likely to achieve your goals if you write them down. The act of writing down your goals solidifies them in your thoughts, which will then direct and inspire your actions.

But writing your goals down and "filing" them away somewhere won't help, either. Go online to www.BuildingBrandYou.com to download a printable version of our goal-setting sheet. Fill it out and hang it on your mirror so that you see it every morning when you wake up.

Draft your goals to achieve [You]topia

1. What is your one reason, your main driving force, to stay on track?

Is it creating a better life for your family? Or protecting someone who can't protect himself? Or is it something like seeking adventure and appreciating life?

2. What does [You]topia look like to you? Try to shorten it to two or three easy-to-remember sentences. Keep your notes and the full version to look back on later. This is for quick reference.

3. On your way to [You]topia, what are the true priorities in your life? When faced with a dilemma, you can refer back to your priorities to see what comes first.

4. What values do you hold true to? What gives you a sense of meaning and purpose in life? As ethical and moral decisions arise, you can reference these values to make the right decision for you. List your top five values here.

5. List your top five career goals that will get you to [You]topia. If your end vision includes living in a mansion on the beach, your career goals have to be able to support the income to get you there. However, if you would like to spend more time with your family right now, you might have to live more conservatively or otherwise adjust your income goals.

While you can't change your career overnight, you can start taking the steps to get to your [You]topian career lifestyle by evaluating what you need to get there.

- What will your job title be? CEO of a Fortune 100 company, entrepreneur, or something else?

- What do you have right now that will help you get there?

- What do you need to get there? (education, training, skills, certifications)

- Do you need to pay off any debt or set aside an amount of money to help you get a business started?

- Do you need specific relationships to help you advance in a current job, or land a future job?

6. Set five personal goals to maintain your health - spiritually, emotionally and physically. If your [You]topia includes spending more time with your children or volunteering to mentor children, set a realistic goal of volunteering in a classroom once or twice a month. If you are overwhelmed and overcommitted in life and you need to de-clutter your brain, a more appropriate goal might be to reduce your volunteer work so that you can spend more time on yourself.

Ron Askenas, Senior Partner of Schaffer Consulting, a management-consulting firm, wrote about the seven mistakes leaders make in setting goals. These mistakes were written for a corporate setting - but the lessons can be applied to your own personal goal setting practice.

1. **Backing away from tough expectations:** You spend more time negotiating the goal downward than in figuring out how to achieve it.

2. **Engaging in charades:** You and your people know from the beginning that the goal is just an exercise to convey the appearance of progress, but there's no hope of achieving it.

3. **Accepting seesaw trades:** When your people take on one goal, they are relieved of another one.

4. **Setting vague or distant goals:** The time frame is not explicitly defined or set too far into the future, so no one takes it seriously.

5. **Not establishing consequences:** You don't really differentiate between those who successfully achieve goals and those who do not.

6. **Setting too many goals:** By assigning an overabundance of objectives you allow subordinates to pick and choose the goals that they either want to do or find easiest to do — but not necessarily the ones that are most important.

7. **Allowing deflection to preparations, studies, and research:** You allow people to spend time planning instead of committing to a real goal.

WHAT IS YOUR ONE REASON TO STAY ON TRACK?	
DESCRIBE [YOU]TOPIA	

TRUE PRIORITIES	VALUES
1.	1.
2.	2.
3.	3.
4.	4.
5.	5.

TOP 5 CAREER GOALS	TOP 5 PERSONAL GOALS
1.	1.
2.	2.
3.	3.
4.	4.
5.	5.

YOUR NOTES

CHAPTER NINE

3. Value Brand [You] or no one else will

"The primary focus of your brand message must be on how special you are, not how cheap you are. The goal must be to sell the distinctive quality of the brand."
Kerry Light, brand strategist.

Too often, businesses and professionals undercut their own value when they don't ask for that raise, work excessive hours or otherwise deeply discount a consulting fee. If you allow the discussion to focus on discounted price, you've already lost your brand value.

Your customers will never appreciate your service because they never did. They grudgingly accepted your cheap price. Even if you deliver exactly what you promise to deliver, they will never be satisfied with their bills. And when the next cheap trick comes around, they will move on.

For example, businesses can enjoy a lot of exposure when they capitalize on the power of group buying through sites such as Groupon and Living Social. But, how often have you returned to buy something at full price after you bought it for 50 to 70 percent off?

Promotions and discount offers can be a useful part of a marketing budget, but should never be the primary introduction.

In order to build Brand Value, you need to:

1) Know who your customer is and why they value you

2) Equip yourself with the right tools to provide top-notch customer service

3) Focus on delivering the value that your customers desire

"Brands are confusing brand love with brand attention - giving people cheap gifts might keep them on the radar but it won't grow affection for the future," Tiffany Kenyon, planning director at Ogilvy & Mather.

In fact, cheap gimmicks can close your doors...

After an eight-year run, an Italian restaurant with a unique flavor that had received national recognition was forced to abruptly shut its doors and go out of business.

With a self-described "American Neapolitan" menu, this restaurant leveraged Italian-style cooking with local ingredients. The restaurant featured a high-end wine bar, decadent appetizers and a signature lasagna that received rave reviews in national magazines.

This was a luxury brand with a dedicated following of retired couples with money willing to pay premium prices for the experience of sharing a multi-course meal and lingering for long conversations over perfectly decanted wines.

As social-media marketing peaked for small businesses in 2008 and 2009, the restaurant aggressively sought Facebook fans and hosted Tweetups in an ideal location midway between two metropolitan markets. In their zeal to grow fans, the restaurant began offering deep discounts to fans and then started offering "Nickel Lasagna Night", for a cheap version of a dish that was usually priced at $30, with a la carte sides.

Local media applauded the "success" of the restaurant for capitalizing on the newest trend in marketing.

Prior to this shift in marketing, customers were raving about...

"Food Great, made by hand with the freshest and highest quality ingredients (watch them do so) Decor, some of the finest (even though hard to believe from the outside) and the newest wine technology. Oh and one of the finest wine lists in the city. Service was fantastic as well."

"I have eaten here many times and it seems to just keep getting better! It is pricier than Macaroni Grill or Caraba's, {sic} but everything is homemade. Try the truffle ravioli, alder plank tilapia - even the simple cheese ravioli is great. One local tip - sign up your email on their web site as they send discount coupons in the off-season - great value. Definitely one of the top 3 restaurants in town. Great wine selection."

The end result? Reviews like this...

"While this could have been a nice evening, it took over 20 minutes to order drinks, then another 20 before they asked about ordering dinner. This was not at a busy time, it was 9pm at night. By the time the drinks finally arrived, we decided to get the check and go. This was the point the bread showed up. So 45 minutes in, only drinks, no ordering. We got our check and left. The menu looked nice, but pricey. They charge for splitting entrees and appetizers.

Go somewhere where you might get served in a timely manner."

"I have given [this restaurant] several chances, I unfortunately stumbled on a Nickel Lasagna Night, absolute chaos! You may as well go to Olive Garden, no class whatsoever. Do real upmarket restaurants really need to attract customers who are so desperate for cheap pasta."

"I decided to give the restaurant another chance at lunchtime, the food was tasty although portions rather small. The ambiance left something to be desired, the restaurant was very dark and the ceiling made me think I was eating in a warehouse! There was a rather loud obnoxious gentleman shouting in the back of the restaurant, I inquired and was informed it was the owner. "

"My lunch group suggested we go to [this restaurant] for lunch this week, but no we will not be giving them a third chance."

(Reviews taken from restaurant listing on www.NaplesNews.com)

Failing to understand the needs and desires of the restaurant's customer base was the fatal flaw in the marketing plan. This led to marketing efforts that were inconsistent with their premium brand.

While promotions brought in more people for the short-term, those guests only returned for deep discounts and not the premium experience. In the long run, the restaurant repelled the customers who had valued them the most, while attracting those they valued the least.

You can avoid this mistake by taking the time to identify your Ideal Customer and understanding why they value your service or product. You'll learn more about profiling your Ideal Customer in chapter 10.

"Your premium brand had better be delivering something special, or it's not going to get the business," Warren Buffett, billionaire business executive and investor.

Brand value can also be shaken when employees don't have the most basic needs to provide superior service to a customer.

I have been a brand cheerleader for Delta for several years, after their staff went above and beyond to assist me while I was traveling with my young daughter. Their slogan, "We love to fly and it shows," rang true on a seventeen-hour trip.

However, my confidence was shaken during a business trip. Returning home on a cross-country red-eye flight, I boarded the plane to hear the First-Class flight attendants complaining about not having the space or supplies to do their jobs.

The flight and the food service were fine until I asked for a second cup of tea. The flight attendant said she would be happy to get me a cup of hot water for my tea if she could find a cup. Delta had rationed out the little foam cups and she thought they were out. Eventually, she found one and gave it to me. As a customer, it was embarrassingly awkward to feel like such a simple request for a cup of hot water was so difficult to fulfill.

While the flight attendants were as polite as ever, they were not confidently equipped to provide the level of service that was expected of them.

And it certainly did not live up to Delta's new slogan that they "are in the business of Up" and that they are raising the bar on flying.

As you build your brand, make sure that you equip yourself with the right tools to provide your customers with the best customer service possible. It could be preparing yourself with a notepad to take notes, using a cell phone carrier with good reception, or making sure that your computer software is comparable to your clients so that they don't have to convert files for you.

In all fairness to Delta, I did submit feedback about the incident on their website. They responded very quickly with an apology for the poor customer service, appreciation for the comments and some bonus miles for my account to make up for the service. The speed of their response (within twenty-four hours) was extraordinary and the tone of the letter was genuine.

When was the last time that Disney offered you a discount?

On one (of many) trips to Disney World, my then four-year-old daughter wanted to see the princesses. Two hours into the line I begged her to come back later, but she held fast. She wanted to see the princesses. The vein in my forehead was ready to explode from all the crying children around us, but my patient daughter excitedly waited for her turn.

Then, as we approached the final stretch, she asked for her autograph book and promptly started to sign her name. I asked what she was doing and she said that she needed to show the princess her name.

Magical Disney moment started…

Then she showed her name to the princesses, who proceeded to write special notes with her and made her feel like the only child there. She didn't just walk out of that room; she floated on air with eyes glowing as big as the moon.

POOF

Magical Disney moment delivered...

I forgot all about the wait in line and the hefty expense of purchasing tickets to get into the park and all of the princess gear.

> *"A brand is a living entity - and it is enriched or undermined cumulatively over time, the product of a thousand small gestures,"* Michael Eisner, former chief executive officer of The Walt Disney Company (1984-2005).

Disney executives understand the value of their brand isn't in the $85 ticket; it is in their ability to deliver an individualized magical experience to millions of guests each and every day of the year. From the pristinely manicured Main Street USA, to perfectly timed fireworks complete with Tinker Bell's flight at 10 pm, sharp, they have to deliver magic because that is the value that their customers desire.

Do you think this massive cast of characters would be able to deliver the "Disney Experience" if their foam cups were rationed out to the first 100,000 guests? Would dining in Cinderella's Castle be such a treat if they offered "Nickel Lasagna Night"?

How do you evaluate skills, accomplishments, strengths and weakness to develop your Brand Value?

Before your customers can appreciate the real value of Brand [You], you must be able to accurately understand and confidently express the value you bring to the relationship.

Every public relations campaign starts with (or should start with) research and a situational analysis to understand what message would most effectively resonate with our target audience. We want to inventory your best assets and make a critical assessment of skills and tools that you need to achieve your brand.

Now is not the time to be modest or humble. In the words of Barney Stinson, a character from the television show, "How I Met Your Mother": "It is time to suit up!"

Take a minute to think about your top accomplishments of all time. These would be the things that make you most proud.

- Did you overcome adversity?

- Did you help a charity raise funds?

- Did you inspire someone to change?

Certainly, getting married or having children are proud moments in time, but unless you advanced science and human rights by bioengineering your spouse from a cell, that isn't the kind of moment we are talking about. Right now, we are focusing on your marketable skills and talents.

Also, think about your significant accomplishments or contributions. Showing up on time, organizing the files on your desk and sharpening your pencils efficiently don't count.

- How did you increase profits?

- How did you bring together a team?

- How did you earn that prestigious award?

What are your top five accomplishments of all time?

1. _____

2. _____

3. _____

4. _____

5. _____

I'm sure you've done a lot more than five great things in your lifetime. You should list all of those on your resume so that people can understand the depth and breadth of your career.

However, in building your brand, we have to cut through the clutter to the most important and special elements that set you apart from everyone else and translate them into benefits for your employer and/or customer. We are honing in on your top five accomplishments so that you can focus on the best of the best.

Now, let's take your top five accomplishments and make them more meaningful and relevant by translating them into benefits for your customers.

Get emotional with your accomplishments.

Maybe you've walked in the Relay for Life for the past ten years. It is meaningful for you, but you may be overlooking the impact that you've had on your community with a simple statement like...

- "I walked in the Relay for Life..."

Be specific about your accomplishments so that you can understand the broader emotional impact of what you've been able to do and convey your passion.

- "Last year, I organized a team of fifteen of my co-workers to walk in the Relay for Life. Together, we raised more than $5,000 to help end cancer. This is my tenth year participating in the Relay for Life and over the years, I have helped raise awareness about the American Cancer Society and brought together a support group that was able to help Betty when she had cancer this year…"

Potential benefits that this accomplishment conveys:

- You are a team builder who can rally a group around my business.

- You understand the value of results in raising funds.

- You are loyal or committed to seeing a project through because you have participated for ten years.

- You are compassionate about your colleagues.

Look at the bigger picture of your contributions.

It is easy for business development professionals to set sales and see that they achieved $1 million in gross revenues. But, sometimes, in an administrative position, it is harder to see the impact of your accomplishments.

- "I manage customer files…"

Managing your customer files has an impact on productivity and the ability to serve clients. Your accomplishment could easily have a broader impact than you realize.

- "Last year, I reorganized the customer filing system so that executive staff and sales managers could easily identify past orders and repeat customers to pro-actively reach out for additional sales. With this increased productivity, we have seen our customer response time reduced, customer satisfaction reports are more positive and repeat sales have increased."

Potential benefits that this accomplishment conveys:

- You will take initiative on projects and stay organized so that your customer doesn't have to micromanage you.

- You can save me hours of time and frustration by developing a system that lets me focus on what I do best.

- You are going to help me grow by keeping my customers happy

Don't forget the sales mantra WiiFM - "What's in it for me?"

Lesson No. 1 in all sales training courses is that people don't buy features, they buy benefits that help them feel good or avoid negative repercussions. When you walk onto a car lot and head straight for the red cars, it isn't because red paint is more durable than blue paint. You walk to the red paint because it makes you feel good. In a sales position, you might describe a simple sales figure.

- "I sold 100 cars last year..."

The salesperson who can hone in on exactly the benefits that his customers are looking for will make a lot more money.

- "Last year I helped more than 100 business professionals, who were also weekend warriors, find the perfect vehicle that projected the right image at work and gave them the flexibility for every weekend adventure they were looking for. If you have a few minutes, I'd like to help you find the right car to help you get the most out of your lifestyle."

Potential benefits that this accomplishment conveys:

- You will listen to my customers' needs and help them find the right solutions.

- You know how to build trust.

Now, hone your top five accomplishments and translate them into the benefits that you bring to the table.

TOP 5 ACCOMPLISHMENTS	TRANSLATED INTO BENEFITS
1.	1.
2.	2.
3.	3.
4.	4.
5.	5.
BRAND VALUE STATEMENT:	

Summarize your five benefits statements into one sentence. What value do you bring to your business relationships?

Brand value statement:

_____

_____

_____

Do your proudest accomplishments connect with your passion in life? Will they help you get to [You]topia?

Andrew Davis, author of *Brandscaping: Unleashing the Power of Partnerships*, believes that people mistakenly substitute their education and background for their passion, which leaves them as a basic and disposable commodity. "However, when individuals marry their passion with their experience and education they immediately differentiate themselves. For example, a graphic designer with a passion for skateboards is infinitely more valuable to those brands that are pursuing skateboarders."

By definition, a brand is only going to be valuable to a certain targeted audience. It may as well be people who appreciate your passion in life, value your services and are willing to pay for it.

Brand [You] Lessons:

1) Know who your customers are and why they value you

2) Equip yourself with the right tools to provide top-notch customer service

3) Focus on delivering the value your customers desire

"You do not build brand value by saying how cheap you are. You do build brand value by reinforcing how special you are," Larry Light, chief executive officer of Arcature, LLC and author of "Six Rules for Brand Revitalization".

YOUR NOTES

CHAPTER TEN

4. BUILD YOUR NETWORK WISELY

On any given day of the week, you can easily find a half-dozen networking events that might have *some* contacts you could *probably* meet. Attending all of those events will certainly leave you feeling as though you've worked a lot, but won't necessarily propel you to your goals.

Working with multiple executives on very tight schedules, I've found that they spent as much as twenty to thirty hours a week at business-related networking events. They were well-known by the networking circuit, but they weren't generating any tangible results from those events to help build their businesses.

As you have (I hope) realized, two themes run through this book:

1) *Cut through the Clutter*

2) *Develop Targeted Trust*

If you try to be everything to everyone, you'll end up running in circles and constantly trying to catch up with the obligations that you've made. Precious, valuable, billable time is wasted explaining who you are to yet another group of people who are going to "pick your brain" for ideas and move on because they are simply not ready to make a real investment in your expertise.

To cut through the clutter and develop a solid customer base that will push Brand [You] into success, you need to think strategically about the relationships you build so you can carve out your profitable niche.

"If you are going to be an industry leader, you need to know your niche. In what area can you be most impactful?" said Joe Pulizzi, author and founder of Content Marketing Institute.

With a deliberate approach, you can easily manage your relationships and your networking time by segmenting your contacts into three groups:

1) *Ideal Customers*

2) *Network of Peers*

3) *Inspirational Relationships*

Focusing your time and efforts on these three groups of relationships will help you confidently evaluate if an event or a relationship is worth pursuing, by asking yourself:

- Will this networking group or association connect me to my ideal customers?

- Does this network of peers help me grow and challenge me to enhance my skills?

- Do these individuals inspire me to be a better person?

It is as easy as yes or no. If the answer is yes, it is worth pursuing. If the answer is no, you can confidently make a decision to decline the opportunity and spend your time on something more enriching for you.

If you find that you are rationalizing, thinking "this might be a good place to meet someone...", then you could easily find yourself with another twenty to thirty hours of obligations to networking groups that get you nowhere. It is wiser to set the "might be good" events or groups to the side. If you have extra time or find them more useful at a later time, you can always attend.

As we break your relationships into three core groups, we are hoping to give you the right support system, generate more business and keep you personally fulfilled. At different times in your career, you may need to focus on developing one particular group of contacts. To achieve the lifestyle you desire, you need to have a sensible distribution of all three types of relationships.

Leaning too heavily on your Inspirational Relationships may create financial challenges. On the flip side, working too hard trying to generate sales through your Ideal Customers may eventually leave you drained and unfulfilled.

Our goal is to find a synergistic balance of the relationships. Some relationships will stand alone, but in our blending lives, you will also find that some of these relationships intersect. Some of your Ideal Customers may turn into Inspirational Relationships, Peer Network to Ideal Customers, or maybe you are lucky to have a few relationships that fall into all three segments.

That is great news!

Hopefully, that means you are waking up every morning to do something you love (some form of work) with people who you respect and admire. Identify and recognize these special relationships so that you can focus your time and energy on helping each other grow.

Building the right relationships

In 2002, I found myself working at a construction company called PBS Contractors. One day, I was driving to an appointment with the owner, Russell Budd. He asked me why I had chosen to work with the company.

I explained that in the interview process, I just "clicked" with the individuals. And I was really impressed that most of the employees had been with him for more than five years and some for more than twenty.

He chuckled and said "So, you thought that we couldn't suck too bad!"

Thus, the start of a great relationship.

An Ideal Customer / Employer

I respect Russell because he encourages everyone to speak up about ideas for improvement and truly listens to all of them. He doesn't always agree, but he always actively listens and shows how much he values and respects the person's opinion. He encourages his team to grow, learn and better themselves - hoping that will make the entire company better even knowing that some of the rising stars will eventually leave.

Inspirational Friend

When Russell's children were young, they used to come into the office and leave yellow sticky notes all over his office. He had a wall covered with little sheets of yellow paper saying "I Love You" and "You are the BEST dad ever".

At the time, he was famous for cancelling business lunches so that he could have lunch with his children at school. Russell would say, "Ten years from now, you won't remember that meeting or networking event that you missed. But you will remember the smile on your kids' faces and maybe... just maybe... they will too."

Perfect Peer

Years later, when it came time to start my business, I turned to someone I trusted and admired. Though we had a similar thought process, we had different vantage points for the solution. He was able to offer a unique perspective and offer invaluable insights. Russell is one of my most trusted confidants and advisors.

More than a decade later, I can laugh and agree that neither Russell Budd nor PBS Contractors "sucked" at all. I am a better person all-around for taking the time to build this relationship.

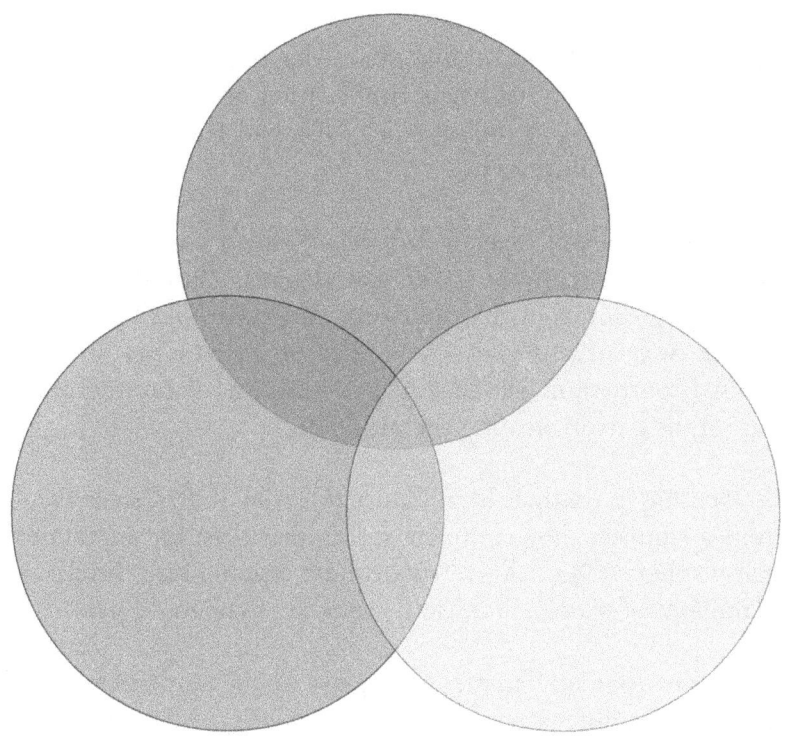

Take some time to explore your existing relationships. How would they fit into these three core groups?

Ideal Customers

Your Ideal Customer is the person with whom everything seems to flow. You are a good personality match, the value you offer is understood, and you look forward to hearing from this person.

Learn everything you can about your Ideal Customers and how you can connect with them. Which groups do they belong to? What hobbies do they have? Which magazines do they read?

What are they thinking about when they use your product? On an emotional level, what is pushing them while they use your product or service?

In the 1970s and 1980s, Nike was struggling to compete with Reebok, a company that had nimbly jumped on the emerging aerobics trend. As a "running shoe", Nike had a limited customer base of marathon runners.

In 1988, Nike's ad agency Wieden+Kennedy, came up with one of the company's best known slogans, "Just do it". The advertising campaign that followed, and even Nike's corporate culture, was infused with "...the idea of the intense, inwardly focused competitor. The ads rarely focused on the product itself, but on the person wearing the product."

By focusing in on their Ideal Customer, Nike shifted their brand from a running shoe company to a sports shoe for any athlete that wanted to "Just do it," successfully tapping into the desires of millions of people, increasing its market share to 43 percent. [10]

From the football fanatic who plays to be remembered, to inspiring the inner strength of female athletes, to the adventure-seeking weekend warrior, Nike has continued to connect with its Ideal Customers on an emotional level by understanding their truest desires and appealing directly to them.

"We used to put the brand in the middle. Now the consumer is smack-dab in the middle of everything we do. And that means we need to understand who our customer is," said Joaquin Hidalgo, vice president and general manager of Emerging Markets at Nike.

When you know exactly who your Ideal Customer is, you can focus your branding efforts in the right networking places.

Some people mistakenly think that building awareness means investing a lot of time and a lot of money in association memberships. They assume that membership alone will provide exposure and generate business. But, the truth is, investing your time in the right association and building genuine relationships within the right network will get you much farther than ten memberships you don't have time to use.

When one of my clients, Dave, took the time to evaluate his networking groups, he found he was spending up to twenty hours a week volunteering with an organization that generated less than 5 percent of his business, while he was investing a just few hours a month in an association that was generating more than 20 percent of his business.

On a day-to-day basis, he felt busy with the first group, but hadn't sat down to evaluate results. Once he saw where his best customers were coming from, it was crystal clear where he should be investing his time. He made the switch and, after six months, his sales figures jumped by double digits, confirming that he had made the right choice.

For start-up companies on a shoestring budget, you can develop a referral network by simply focusing on relationships and brand partnerships.

As a brand consultant, Andrew Davis knew exactly who his Ideal Customer was - newly appointed chief marketing officers at mid-size technology companies and financial institutions. When he launched Tippingpoint Labs, he also knew he wasn't going to meet enough of his Ideal Customers at the average networking meeting, trade association or chamber of commerce. With a finite amount of time and a budget to consider, he looked for the best way to get a warm introduction to this type of customer.

He started identifying non-competing businesses with an established customer base and a solid brand reputation. With this target list in hand, he started calling the individuals within the businesses.

"In the early days, we built our professional network by going into meetings with the goal of developing mentor relationships. We hoped to gain advice on how to best serve our customers," said Davis. "Our ideal customers came out of casual conversations and brainstorming sessions for client projects."

Take a minute to write down your top five Ideal Customers:

- Who are they?

- What are some of their common characteristics?

- To which groups do they belong?

- Which charities do they care about?

- What can you do to improve your existing relationships, or make new ones?

- What is the single most important networking group or association that you need to belong to so that you can meet more of your Ideal Customers?

_____

_____

_____

_____

_____

Network of Peers

Many business professionals question the value of networking with anyone they perceive as competitors. You must understand the distinct difference between competitors and peers.

Your peers may work in the same industry, but they aren't looking to steal your business away. Your peers are a support network that helps you grow professionally. By discussing ideas and learning best practices, you will keep your skills sharp and fresh, so that you can provide the best service.

With a strong Brand [You] in place, your network of peers may turn into one of your best referral sources. Why would they send business to you? Your business peers can't serve every customer. And when they need to make a referral, wouldn't they send the business to someone they trust?

How do you handle competitors?

Trust is a two-way street. If you find yourself guarded among a group of industry professionals, you need to figure out what the real problem is.

Are they truly cut-throat competitors who are only looking to steal your contacts and throw you under the bus?

Chartered in 1947, the Public Relations Society of America (PRSA) is the world's largest organization of public relations professionals. PRSA provides professional development, sets the standards of excellence in the industry and upholds principles of ethics for its members and the multi-billion dollar global public relations profession.

In a highly competitive and creative industry, there are public relations professionals who choose to avoid their "competitors" and organizations such as PRSA.

However, PRSA is able to bring together a network of more than 21,000 peers who share common goal of Advancing the Profession and the Professional. Members are represented in a cross section of 111 Chapter, 10 Districts and 14 Professional Interest Sections to share expertise and best practices.

"Professional associations offer one of best ways to network. Here at PRSA, our members have an opportunity to showcase their talents while they learn, teach, give back, and benefit from other professionals. Whether virtually or in person, locally or nationally or within an area of specialization, PRSA makes connecting easy," William Murray, CAE, president and chief operating officer for the Public Relations Society of America.

Chances are, this is not the case. Most individuals I've met who feel this way about peer groups are personally insecure in their relationships with their customers. Even if someone stole your entire Rolodex of contact names and phone numbers, your relationships could never be replicated.

The big question is, do you have a solid relationship with an ideal and loyal customer? Have you taken time to develop the trust and reputation as a results-oriented individual?

When you are with your network of peers, your focus should be on finding ways to learn and share ideas so that you can improve your industry together. By sharing in educational and advocacy initiatives, you can help each other serve your employer, and/or your customers, more effectively.

However, if you truly find yourself in a den of thieves, you are, obviously, among the wrong group of people. Politely excuse yourself and start looking for your next peer group.

Your peer groups can also take the form of mentors, masterminds, or a brain trust of professionals who offer expertise in an area that you lack. These don't have to be formal mentorship programs, they can just be trusted friends who will give you honest feedback and push you a little harder than you would push yourself.

Joe Pulizzi, author and founder of Content Marketing Institute, credits one of his mentors -- a business-savvy venture capitalist -- for giving him a much needed wake-up call.

Pulizzi was comfortable with how his business was growing and thought he was staying ahead of his competition. One morning, he got a call from his mentor, who bluntly told Pulizzi that his main competitor was rapidly passing him by. His mentor said it was time to "put it all on the line and place the flag in the ground, come hell or high water."

That wake-up call inspired Pulizzi to take the Content Marketing Institute to the next level by refocusing his strategy to successfully stay ahead of the competition.

Take a minute to write down your Network of Peers:
- Who are they?
- Where do you connect with them most effectively?
- What do you learn from them?
- Moving forward, what do you need to learn from them?
- Do you need to find a peer group or mentor?

_____

_____

_____

_____

_____

Inspirational Relationships

One of the biggest issues that high-ranking business executives, elected officials and celebrities deal with is living a very public life. The pressure to be "ON", to say the right thing, and always be ready to give the right solution, can be overwhelming and exhausting.

You need time to laugh, play, and let your guard down.

Inspirational people aren't just the people you run to when you have a bad day. Developing and maintaining a real connection to your inspirational relationships will leave you feeling energized on your path to [You]topia. You will have fewer bad days because you are surrounding yourself with positive people who believe in you, not just people who drain you because they need something.

When you do have the occasional bump in the road, the inspirational people are the ones who help pull you out of the funk.

Who falls into your inspirational relationships?

- Family
- Close friends
- Volunteer or service-based groups
- Religious groups
- Fitness groups/Fitness friends
- Hobby organizations

While inspirational figures, such as Ghandi, Martin Luther King, Jr. or a celebrity, are positive role models, they aren't true relationships because you can't connect with them. Your inspirational relationships should be people with whom you feel a strong personal connection. They see you for who you are and are proud to know you. You can let your guard down, whether you need to laugh or cry.

Avoid energy vampires and obliged relationships

There are many social obligations in our lives, from events with family members to the occasional happy hour with your co-workers. It is easy to justify those obligations as requirements for being part of the team. But is it the right team for you? Don't fall prey to these misguided "shoulds":

- You should go visit... *that friend or relative who is overly critical and whose life is fuelled by one emotional tornado after the next...*

- You should go to that church... *because it is the "right" church and if you don't, you'll go to Hell...*

- You should join... *any one of a thousand volunteer groups that has weekly service project you don't have time or money to do...*

- You should... *go have a drink with your co-workers to commiserate about the long work day, how little you get paid and how underappreciated you all are...*

When relationships consistently leave you feeling guilty, drained and beat up, they distract you from your goals. At best, you lose a couple of hours of your day. At worst, you end up constantly being distracted by things other than your goals and the relationships that are truly important to you.

As you move toward your goals, take a long, hard look at the people who surround you. Do they help lift you up? Or are they cutting you down?

Donald Trump says you should dress for the job you want, not the job you have. I believe that the same is true in relationships. You should surround yourself with people who are where you want to be in life, as customers, peers, and inspirational contacts.

When you surround yourself with people who are positive influences, you will naturally absorb lessons from their experiences and stay motivated on your path to Brand [You].

Take a minute to write down your top five Inspirational Relationships:

- Who are they?

- What are some of their common characteristics?

- How often do you talk to or see them?

- What can you do to improve your existing relationships or make new ones?

_____

_____

_____

_____

_____

How balanced are groups of relationships?
Is there one group you need to focus on developing right now?

_____

_____

_____

_____

_____

The key to turning contacts into relationships

Whether you are maintaining relationships with existing contacts or looking to bring new people into your circles of influence as Ideal Customers, Network of Peers, or Inspirational Relationships, you need a plan for managing those relationships. Turning contacts into relationships starts with a genuine interest in building relationships.

"Make time to build relationships. They will be your best source of ideal customers because they understand the value of what you offer," said Andrew Davis, founder of Tippingpoint Labs and author of "Brandscaping".

While there are many contact-management systems with bells and whistles, the best ones still won't make phone calls for you.

If you are looking to turn more of your contacts into relationships, you must make an effort to build a mutually beneficial relationship. That takes some time and thought.

Marketing and advertising studies show that it takes seeing your name seven times for a customer to have enough trust to take action. Solid marketing campaigns seek to touch a customer at least seven times, from strategically placed advertisements, to email, direct mail and special event or community outreach programs.

This theory works in relationships, too. While you may instantly connect with someone at a cocktail party, you certainly won't build a relationship if you don't take the time to reach out to them once in a while. Perhaps there are people you would like to know, but you don't know how to initiate the relationship without sounding as if you are just there to sell something and move on.

In order to build relationships, you need to systemize a series of seven contact points to establish trust and let the other person know you truly want to build a mutually beneficial relationship. You may choose to connect on a social network, telephone call, email or even regular mail. It all depends on your comfort level.

Step 1 - Icebreaker - Once you have identified someone with whom you would like to build a relationship, you need to know where you might be able to break the ice. An icebreaker isn't a lengthy conversation; it is just something to start the conversation.

Are this person a member of a group? Is he or she on LinkedIn? Do you have an email address? Write down the most comfortable way you can break the ice with a potential contact.

One of my clients, PBS Contractors, initiated a "Cookie Program" in marketing to prospective clients. Whenever a prospect made a sale, my client's salespeople would deliver a cookie with a congratulatory note. With a list of about fifteen to twenty stops to make and a $20 weekly cookie budget per salesperson, the program was a simple way to recognize the success of the prospect and introduce the company. In a few short months, the salespeople were being warmly welcomed into offices with comments like, "I know you. I've gotten one of your cookies!"

Step 2 - Introduction - Once you have broken the ice, what is the best way for you to have a more in-depth conversation? Would a fifteen-minute phone call work best? Should you visit the person's office for coffee? Invite the person out to lunch?

Steps 3-6 - Value Add - How can you add value to your prospective contact's day? Perhaps you can forward an article via email, invite the person to speak at one of your peer group meetings, invite them to a charitable event or refer business to them.

SEVEN CONTACT SYSTEM

Now that you've identified the people in the three circles, you can use the Seven Contact System to manage your ongoing relationships and stay on track towards [You]topia.

1.	ICEBREAKER

2.	INTRODUCTION

3.	VALUE ADD

4.	VALUE ADD

5.	VALUE ADD

6.	VALUE ADD

7.	BFF'S

Value doesn't have to come in the form of a forced token of admiration. If it is forced, it may come off as disingenuous and tarnish the relationship altogether. For some of my most cherished relationships, the mutual value is just an energizing conversation about business, politics, or life in general.

"If you're focused on the friendship as its own reward, serendipitous stuff just happens. I know that sounds weird, but I can tell you for our 12 years of existence, it's actually how a lot of stuff happens," said Tony Hsieh, chief executive officer of Zappos.com.[11]

Step 7 - BFF (Best Friend Forever) - You may not be trading friendship bracelets or vacationing together with the family, but at this stage, you have established a trusted relationship. Ideally, you are talking on a semi-regular basis and would have no hesitation about calling to ask for a favor. Depending on where this person fits into your life, you can set up a routine phone call to chat or meeting with an agenda that helps both of you.

- Ideal Customers - Meet occasionally to discuss something other than your contracted business. Learn something personal.

- Network of Peers - Brainstorming sessions can help you both learn.

- Inspirational Relationships - Breakfast or coffee to start the day with a positive outlook.

The most important thing to remember is that both your prospective contacts and existing relationships need to hear from you on a regular basis. And if you want to be an important connection, you have to offer value in these relationships. Do NOT call just to ask for a sale.

YOUR NOTES

CHAPTER ELEVEN

5. BRAND [YOU] MUST BE SIMPLE, SHORT AND STRONG

"There can be as much value in the blink of an eye as in months of rational analysis,"
Malcolm Gladwell, author of
"Blink: The Power of Thinking without Thinking".

In the book "Blink", Malcolm Gladwell explores the concept of "thin-slicing", our ability to interpret and draw a conclusion based on a limited amount of detailed information. Of course, this interpretation of a thin-slice is shaped by our own internal expertise, intuition, prejudices and stereotypes, conscious or unconsciously.

Gladwell illustrates how often having too much information can cloud a person's judgment, leading to a common leadership challenge of paralysis by analysis, the inability to make a decision because of an overload of information. Citing many examples from marketing concepts, to medical accuracy, to predicting the outcome of marriages, Gladwell demonstrates that collecting additional facts, figures and details often just reinforces your initial interpretation without making it more accurate.

What does this mean for Brand [You]?

First impressions are another type of thin slice, where people are making decisions about you based on extremely limited information. The impression that you leave is more than important, it can mean the difference between being given an opportunity or getting passed over as just another face in the crowd. When people thin-slice you, make sure they find someone they want to get to know more in-depth.

While your first impression may get you in the door, you have to be prepared to back it up with real substance by effectively communicating your expertise, knowledge and relevance to your potential customer or employer. Many professionals with real value lose the deal or the relationship because they cloud the message with irrelevant details that mean nothing to their potential customers.

In communicating Brand [You], you have to make a positive first impression and effectively communicate your value and relevance by:

- Polishing your appearance and body language

- Organizing a clear, concise key messages to communicate

- Illustrating your key messages with easy to understand stories

- Making your message more relevant by focusing on your audience and speaking in their language

- Leaving people feeling confident, inspired and in charge

Polish your appearance and body language

"When you meet someone for the first time, or walk into a house you are thinking of buying, or read the first few sentences of a book, your

mind takes about two seconds to jump to a series of conclusions," says Malcolm Gladwell.

Studies confirm that 93 percent of how you are judged is based on nonverbal indicators, your physical appearance and your body language.

Meet "Dick" & "Jane"

- What are your honest impressions of Dick & Jane?

- What level of career have they achieved? Are they going to continue to grow in their career?

- Do they look competent or reliable? If you needed to get an important job done, would you trust either one of them to get it done correctly?

- Do they look happy in either their career or personal lives?

When you look sloppy, unkempt, and stressed out, all that people can see are the flaws in your appearance. Those flaws superimpose as flaws in your personality and your ability to succeed. It is the equivalent of hiding behind a tattered stage curtain in life, where no one can possibly see your potential.

Dressing appropriately, whether that is a pair of scrubs, jeans and a hardhat, or a tailored three-piece suit isn't a vain attempt to impress people. When you dress appropriately for the career that you want, you will exude confidence in who you are and where you are going. Instead of noticing the flaws in your attire (and perceived flaws in you), people will notice the feeling of confidence, comfort and professionalism they are left with after meeting you.

If you are like many professionals (myself included) who have a hard time putting together a look off the shelf, a consultation with a personal stylist is worth the investment because you will have help coordinating a closet full of clothing that will help you feel confident.

Some executives may pay hundreds of dollars an hour for a personal stylist consultation, but many upscale clothing retailers, such as Nordstrom and Dillard's, offer a complimentary personal shopping service for both men and women.

With these style specialists, you'll gain a new understanding of the types of clothing that flatter your body type and give a healthier glow by complementing your skin tone. A stylist's job is to take your wardrobe from good to great by purchasing some key essentials in flattering shapes, adding in your personality and making you shine.

You may pay a few more dollars for some key clothing pieces, but it will be more than worth it as you start using more of your wardrobe instead of wasting precious resources on clothing that you just don't like and don't wear.

After you refresh your closet, it will be time to take a critical look at your body language to make sure you are sending out the right message.

Body language for Brand [You]

Getting ahead in both your personal and professional life involves building relationships based on mutual trust. In an ideal world, people would say exactly what they mean so you can react honestly.

In the real world, it pays to be conscious of both your body-language messages, and to be sensitive enough to read between the lines and interpret the real message you are receiving from those around you.

If you are trying to build new relationships, but you are regularly making some of the following body language mistakes, how successful do you think you will be?

Common body language mistakes

BAD HABITS	THE MESSAGE YOU ARE SENDING
Avoiding eye contact	You are disinterested
Slouching	You lack confidence or have poor self esteem
Folding your arms across your chest	You are closed off and disinterested in what the person is saying
Frequently looking down	You are uncomfortable or self-conscious
Angling your body away from others or angling your feet away from others	You are looking to get away from the person
Fidgeting or playing with your hair	You are uncomfortable or anxious
Glancing at the clock	You are disinterested in the conversation or arrogant
Frowning, scowling or scrunching your eyebrows	You are defensive or disagree with the conversation
Leaving your phone visible, texting or checking email during a conversation	You don't think that the person you are with is important

Consciously removing these bad habits from your body language will certainly help you get ahead. However, in building Brand [You], you need to make a more concerted effort to take notice of these valuable messages that are overlooked by your average professional.

Poor body language landed Mark Pincus, Zynga's CEO and founder, on Decker Communication's list of Top Ten Worst Communicators for 2012.

> "His body language distracts from his words. Arms crossed, smug smile - even his tone is condescending. Pincus comes across as arrogant and aloof, with eyes darting away as if there's somewhere he'd rather be. It's hard to connect to him."[12]

International best-selling author, speaker and body language expert Joe Navarro has forty-five years of experience studying body language, including twenty-five years as an FBI Counterintelligence Officer. In his book, "What Every Body is Saying", Navarro explains that accurately speed reading a person's true intentions is a rich and rewarding way to build trust with your colleagues and your friends.

After all, if you can successfully, read someone's true intentions and respond appropriately, you will leave that person relieved and comfortable around you. By taking the time to read between the lines, you will engender trust, which will ultimately build your brand and brand value.

Among Navarro's tips in "What Every Body is Saying" are four essential tips that will help set you above the rest in reading and responding to your clients and colleagues:

>   **1) You must open your eyes to what is around you.** Often while listening, we are distracted from the message by trying to think of our next response. The same is true with the eyes. It is easy to see without observing the true intentions.

>   **2) Feet don't lie.** While many people watch the face for reactions, Navarro says that we have been trained to deceive from an early age when our parents tell us to "put on the happy face" under less-than-happy circumstances. But,

thanks to our internal instincts and the fight-or-flight response system, the feet are more accurate. By noticing if a prospect has an aggressive, fighter's stance or is turned away as if looking for an escape, you can diffuse the potentially negative situation and come back at a later time.

3) Pacifiers may indicate that your client, colleague or employer is uncomfortable with your discussion or the situation. Watch for signs like someone hugging herself, pulling at the neck of a shirt, touching or rubbing the face, pulling at the earlobe, or rubbing open hands downward on the thighs. If you see any of these non-verbal responses, be proactive in changing the course of the conversation. Ask the person questions that might help understand the root cause and find the right solution.

It could be as simple as "Is there something about this project you would change?" OR "Do you have any ideas that could make this better?"

By being responsive to these non-verbal cues, the person you are with will be grateful for the opportunity to open up.

4) Being more expressive with your hand movements will enhance your credibility and persuasiveness. The more expressive your hands are, the more it conveys honesty and enthusiasm which will naturally enhance your brand value and attract people to you.

On the other hand, hiding your hands or keeping them unnaturally still leaves a negative impression of distrust. Standing with your hands behind your back also sends a signal of "don't approach me". If you are unapproachable, your brand will certainly suffer.

It doesn't matter if your uniform is a Gucci suit or a lab coat; you have to take the time to care about your physical appearance by dressing appropriately and consciously using positive body language. When you are comfortable and confident in your appearance and your body language, people will naturally gravitate toward you as someone they need to know.

In addition to sending the right signals with your own body language, you have to be aware of what you are receiving. When you are in conversation with someone, be aware of both positive and negative body language so that you can respond appropriately. With your "intuitive" response, your contacts will be appreciative of your response, comfortable around you and more confident in working with you.

Next time you are at a networking event, lunch or business meeting, focus on one person's body language. What is he or she telling you about their interest via their body language?

When are you meeting with one of your friends, colleagues, or Brain Trust members? Ask them about bad body language habit that you have and decide if you are going to fix it.

Organize clear, concise key messages to communicate

If you look at some of the nation's best communicators from recent years -- Apple founder Steve Jobs, New Jersey Gov. Chris Christie, former President Bill Clinton, Facebook' COO Sheryl Sandberg, and even celebrity Steven Colbert -- you will notice they have different personalities, styles and mediums that they work across.

When you listen to one of these people speaking, one on one or in a public setting, they come across authentic, prepared and confident leaders in their field.

How do they come across so effectively?

They understand a topic and distill it down into specific, bite-sized, and easily understandable key messages.

On the other hand, when you fail to prepare, you could end up looking like Vice President Joe Biden (2008-2016), who is probably best known for his ongoing gaffes. He is a friendly guy who just keeps smiling and talking while he continues to lose all credibility.

Crafting the right key messages

Key messages are simple, easily understood, short messages that you want people to know about you. Typically, your key messages should be influential in nature, not a cold hard fact or figure.

In crafting key messages, you have to balance your need to express a message with what the recipient needs to know in his or her day-to-day life. Your messages must be concise and compelling, making it easy for people to understand and focus on the specific issues you want them to know.

In life (as well as presentations), you should have about three to five key messages ready to employ. If you start sharing more than five, you will lose your audience with too much information and you will lose the value and clarity of your brand. Your key messages should express:

1) You are an influencer because you have a vivid vision of your [You]topia

2) Establish credibility with your top five accomplishments

3) Relevance and "What is in it for me" (WiiFM) through your benefits statements

4) Your brand value

5) What action would you like people to take?

You are an influencer because you have a vivid vision of your [You]topia

As we discussed in chapter 5, your [You]topia is a clear vision of your ideal future. Simply knowing where you want to be in your life allows you to take a first step in establishing your influence. Instead of spinning in circles with the majority of people, it will be obvious to others that you are on a distinct course in life. You've set your direction and are on your way. People will either jump on board or get out of your way.

This key message of you and your vision should be one of the key messages you leave people with when you speak to them one on one, in groups, in publicity and as you conduct yourself.

Rewrite and refine your [You]topia below:

_____

_____

_____

_____

Establish credibility with your top five accomplishments

Chances are, you've met that idealist who has plans to save the world, but can't seem to find his elbow to save his life. Unfortunately, these crackpots mess it up for the rest of us with credible dreams and goals.

The top five accomplishments that we worked through in chapter 7 give your vision credibility because you have already accomplished great things. By communicating your accomplishments -- in the appropriate way -- as one of your key messages, others will have more faith in your ability to get to [You]topia.

Write a summary statement of your top five accomplishments below:

_____

_____

_____

_____

Relevance and "What is in it for me" (WiiFM) through your benefits statements

The third key message you should prepare is crafted around the most important person in the world -- ME! -- also known as your audience of prospective clients and employers. You have to be able to translate your [You]topia and your accomplishments into a message that helps others understand why it is important for "me" to know.

Despite the economic downfall of 2007-2012, many companies and consultants were able to prosper because they could translate their services into WiiFM, meaning, how they could help their potential customers make money, change an image or inspire action. You must be able to connect with people to meet their base needs if your brand is to be relevant.

Write your summary benefits statement below:

_____

_____

_____

_____

Your brand value statement

As we discussed in chapter 9, you have to confidently understand who your customer is and why that customer values your services.

Often the "value" discussion for consultants centers around what is the right rate to charge clients. New consultants often feel compelled to discount their business because they fear losing that first client or because they themselves do not understand the value they bring to the table in a consulting relationship in terms of saving time, saving money, and saving frustration.

Your brand value statement is about more than tasks, it is about solutions that you provide. Write it below:

_____

_____

_____

_____

What action would you like people to take?

This is perhaps the most often overlooked key message in professional development. What action would you like people to take when they meet you? Should they sign up for your blog or email? Should they buy your book or hire you as a consultant? Perhaps they should pledge support to a cause you advocate?

Many professionals fail to close the deal because they fail to ask for the close. The perfect time to direct someone to take action is when you have that person's attention.

Write your action step below:

_____

_____

_____

_____

Understand that these messages will change as you progress through different stages of your career and life, in general. Taking the time to write them down will prepare you with the right messages for any situation, from networking introductions, job or client interviews, or media interviews.

As you draft out your key messages, anticipate potentially tough questions you might have to address, such as explaining gaps on your resume or projects that didn't go as planned. When confronted with potential landmines like this, you should always be open and honest about your role, what you learned and what you did to correct the situation.

Human-resources professionals often tell me they respect candidates more when they show they have taken responsibility for their actions and learned from their mistakes. Recruiters are looking for someone who takes the initiative and learns from mistakes.

"Brands are the express checkout for people living their lives at ever increasing speed," Brandweek.

Illustrating your key messages with easy-to-understand stories

A good story is about more than just entertainment. A good story can help you communicate your key messages in a way that people are more likely to understand and remember.

When we hear facts and figures, our brains decode words into meaning. But that doesn't always translate into something interesting that we need to remember.

Stories engage us more fully in a concept because the decoding process literally engages more of our brains. Our motor cortex lights up as we hear a description of how fast something was. Our sensory cortex lights up as someone describes a smell, touch or taste.

The challenge for you is expressing your five key messages in one or more good stories that are engaging, emotional, genuine and easily retold.

Andrew Davis, author of Brandscaping and famed Muppet Wrangler, suggests that people should think more like television producers and less like marketers by creating a hook that makes the story really interesting.

For example you can tell people that you are a "salesperson", OR you can tell them you are a "weekend warrior and a car consultant".

Which description intrigues you more?

Which one would prompt you to get to know this person more?

Furthermore, Davis said that people mistakenly tend to focus on current experience to give a boring description of what they do right now. In developing that interesting hook, Davis recommends taking inventory of all of your past experience to find a much more memorable, relatable story.

The key to making this relevant is choosing something interesting that compares to your current position and can help transition into the passion that you have for your current position. If you choose a past accomplishment with no relevance to your current position, you run the risk of looking like an out-of-touch has-been.

> On his own resume of fun and interesting jobs, Davis found "Muppet Wrangler" on his list. Through his experience with Jim Henson studios, Davis was able to relate the Muppet Wrangler story to his experience as a brand consultant. Through this interesting hook, he was able to help people understand how branding is very similar to creating and telling a story from the perspective of a television producer. In the process, he was also able to elevate his own personal brand by aligning himself with the success of Jim Henson Studios, a much larger brand to which the general public already relates.

Take your five key messages and think about the stories behind them.

Why are they important to you?

What is the emotional hook they leave you with?

What is unique about the stories that people can easily relate and grab on to?

What about your past experience is extremely memorable, something you are most proud of?

What is your hook?

_____

_____

_____

_____

The best stories come from the heart. If the story you are using to illustrate your key messages doesn't mean anything to you personally, delete it because it will never come across as genuine.

"You've got to find what you love," Steve Jobs, founder of Apple.

Jobs is renowned for the simplicity and ease of Apple's products and the powerfully simple way he could describe the features. Through these product launches, you could easily see into Jobs' personality.

However, a commencement speech that Jobs delivered in 2005[13] to the graduating class at Stanford University was probably the most intensely personal view into his life.

His speech started with:

"Today I want to tell you three stories from my life. That's it. No big deal. Just three stories."

In his minimalist style, Jobs had distilled three stories from his life into three key messages.

Connecting the dots in life - While life might not always make sense at the time, you have to trust that the dots will somehow connect in your future. In a personal look at dropping out of a college degree program and dropping "in" on some elective courses, Jobs described learning about serif and sans serif typefaces in a calligraphy course at Reed College. In this seemingly wasted time, Jobs developed a fascination and appreciation of the beauty of typefaces that lead him to incorporate the typography into the first Mac computer.

"You have to trust that the dots will somehow connect in your future," said Jobs.

Love and loss - Describing the intensely personal and public failure of being fired from his own company, Jobs described how the "heaviness of being successful was replaced by the lightness of being a beginner again." What seemed like an insurmountable loss was actually a door opening into series of more creative and more successful ventures including the start of his next companies NeXT and Pixar.

"Your work is going to fill a large part of your life, and the only way to be truly satisfied is to do what you believe is great work. And the only way to do great work is to love what you do. If you haven't found it yet, keep looking. Don't settle," said Jobs.

Death - Jobs lived his life inspired by the quote "If you live each day as if it was your last, someday you'll most certainly be right." It was a reality check to make sure Jobs was living his life based on what was truly important. After being diagnosed with pancreatic cancer in 2003, Jobs gained a much more personal insight on just how limited your time in this life is and how it should not be wasted living someone else's life.

Jobs left the graduates with a wish to "stay hungry and stay foolish", as they relentlessly pursued their dreams.

What made this speech so memorable?

Jobs took three seemingly unrelated stories and wove them together by illustrating three simple key messages. While he told the stories with revealing detail, the three points were simple and easy to digest. As the graduates left, they probably could not remember all the details of the stories, but they did remember how intensely personal, humorous and emotionally charged they were.

The speech was so powerful that both the video and the transcribed version went viral, leading Stanford University to post the commencement speech in full on its website. A link to the full commencement address is in the reference section of this book.

> As you tell a story, see blocks of time like the scene changes of a play. It will help you remember the sensory and emotional details that will bring the story to life.
>
> Take time to talk as if you are speaking to a friend and give your listeners time to "see" the story, laugh, feel and reflect on the impact.

Focus on your audience and speak their language

In an effort to stand out from the crowd, many people and businesses focus all their efforts on crafting the perfect name. They mistakenly think that the name has to be big, bold and drastically unique, something so unheard of that their ideal customers will be intrigued to ask more about the company name and become customers for life!

The truth is that your brand should stand out for the right reasons. It should be short, easy to understand, and easy to share. It should be visually appealing and avoid potentially offensive insinuations. And, before you take it public, you should always get feedback from a trusted source to ensure it projects the right message.

While a memorable name is important, many of our largest brand names have modest and simple origins.

Brands built on the product names:

"Xerox" is often cited as the perfect example of a brand that stands out because, "Who knows what Xerox means?" The truth is that Xerox is a shortened version of xerography, the process of dry photocopying. Not exactly a sexy or creative origin of a name. In fact, prior to the launch of the first Xerox 914, the company that we now know as Xerox was founded in 1906 as The Haloid Photographic Company.

What about Coca-Cola's landmark branded beverage? The name is a blend of its original two main ingredients, the coca leaf and the kola nut. The epic cola name was a suggestion by developer John Pemberton's bookkeeper, Frank Robinson. Why the two C's? It was thought it would look better in advertising. Reportedly, Pemberton also had excellent penmanship and scripted the familiar and elaborate Spencerian script of the Coca-Cola logo, a characteristic script of the 1880s.

How about a more recent brand, like Google? Google was originally named BackRub because the search engine program was based on checking backlinks that lead into a website, to judge the importance of a site. While it may be technically accurate, the name BackRub has definite negative implications. Thank goodness someone had sense to change the name, but the original plan was to name it Googol, which is the number 10^{100}. While checking availability of the domain name, co-founder Larry Page misspelled the name Google.com. After realizing their mistake, Google executives still liked the name and the rest is history.

Originally founded as Apple Computers, even co-founder Steve Wozniak isn't 100 percent sure of the specific inspiration for the Apple name. It could have been Jobs' stint working at an apple orchard, his love for Apple Records, his love of the fruit, or perhaps a deeper symbolic nature of life and death. Regardless, Wozniak knew there were likely to be a ton of legal issues with trademark. Wozniak and Jobs tried to use alternate names like Executex and Matrix Electronics, but neither were fond of the names so they agreed on Apple.

HARO sought to "Help a Reporter Out". Entrepreneur Peter Shankman built and sold a profitable business based on the simple concept of helping connect reporters and public relations professionals connect.

The Virgin brand name was created during a brainstorming session, in which one of Richard Branson's assistants reportedly commented that "we are virgins in business."

Brands built on the founders' names:

Company brand names are often built around the founder's name:

- Wal-Mart was based on founder Sam Walton

- Ford Motor Company was after founder Henry Ford

- Garmin was named after founders <u>Gary</u> Burrell and Dr. <u>Min</u> Kao

Fashion icon Ralph Lauren was originally born Ralph Lifshitz. He has been credited with changing his name for the success of his business, but the truth is that he changed his name for more pragmatic reasons as a teenager. In an interview with Oprah, Lauren describes a more pragmatic reason for changing his name:

> "My given name has the word shit in it. When I was a kid, the other kids would make a lot of fun of me. It was a tough name. That's why I decided to change it. Then people said, 'Did you change your name because you don't want to be Jewish?' I said, 'Absolutely not. That's not what it's about.' There were also people who thought that because I was Jewish, I had no right to create these preppy clothes. Harvard, Yale, Princeton: 'Why do you like these kind of things?'
>
> My cousins who lived in California had changed their last name to Lawrence. So I just thought, 'I'm going to pick a nice last name'—it wasn't particularly connected to anything or anyone. I was 16, and it was years before I became a designer. It had nothing to do with Jewishness, it had nothing to do with not being proud of who I am. It had to do with not wanting to be at a detriment for no reason in a world that makes fun of things."[14]

Being too creative with your company name can actually backfire and make your brand stumble before you even get out of the proverbial gate. Just ask serial entrepreneur, Joe Pulizzi, who believes that you must keep the message simple enough for people to latch on to easily.

One of his initial companies, "Junta 42", was creative. And the name held a personal and emotionally charged story for Pulizzi. Unfortunately, the company name was difficult to brand for a variety of reasons.

Customers couldn't pronounce it. Was it Juhn-ta or Hoon-ta?

They didn't understand it. Instead of asking what Pulizzi's company could do, customers were asking about the meaning of the name.

Ultimately, they couldn't share it with their friends, which makes the whole concept of word-of-mouth advertising difficult at best.

Pulizzi found the right formula with his company, "Content Marketing Institute" (CMI). As the name implies, the company focuses on providing content marketing strategies to a broad base of subscribers.

"The name worked because it told people exactly what we do. There is no other question, they understand it," said Pulizzi.

I learned a similar lesson in starting my company, which was originally intended to be C^2 Communications. Pronounced C-squared Communications, the company name was cleverly (at least I thought) built around "Content x Connections."

In designing my logo, I wanted a cutting edge feel. While I could clearly see the C^2, many people looked at the logo with a quizzical look on their face. Then they asked, "What is the 'L' stand for?"

My heart sank.

What was so clear and perceptible to me made people stop and stutter. Instead of focusing in on my professional experience as a public relations and marketing expert, they were stuck on a logo and company name they didn't understand. Then the "2" became difficult to place in other forms, so my consulting company morphed to C2 Communications and my ego was only slightly bruised.

My mistake was looking at the logo through my own rose-colored glasses instead of getting feedback from my customers' perspective.

Ultimately, the personal brand that was built on my given name, Cyndee Woolley, trumped my business name anyway. And the unique spelling helped me gain plenty of digital space on all the search engines.

Are you considering establishing a company name? Learn from the best brands.

Your brand name should stand out for the right reasons:

- Be short, easy to understand and easy to share - A Xerox copy is a shortened version of xerography photocopy.

- Be visually appealing - Consider the feel of any signature fonts you use. How will your brand appear? Would it be wise to slightly alter a spelling to make it stand out? Just think, if Coca-Cola hadn't changed the letters in its name, we might be talking about the "Kola" industry today.

- Avoid potentially offensive insinuations - Though a "BackRub" is descriptive of the technological process that Google employs to search backlinks, it certainly isn't the first thing that comes to mind. You might also remove the "shit" from your name as Ralph Lauren did.

- Get feedback from trusted resources - No matter how awesome you think your company name is, get outside opinions. What does the name mean to them? How does it make them feel? What does the color project to them?

In order to effectively communicate Brand [You], you must open the door to the mind with a positive first impression and keep it open by making it easy for people to understand who you are, why you matter and how you can help provide solutions.

"Although we think that decision-making about brands depends strongly on functional benefits, it all comes down to one question: how will this make me feel?" Kim Cramer and Alexander Koene, BR-ND

At the end of the day, your brand isn't what you say it is. Your brand is what people perceive - based on how it makes them feel.

- Are you someone with whom I am comfortable?

- Are you approachable?

- Are you a reliable expert?

- Are you an influential member of the community?

- Will you help me achieve my goals?

Develop a Brand [You] that leaves people feeling confident, inspired and in charge.

YOUR NOTES

CHAPTER TWELVE

6. SMART BRANDS SPEAK UP

For decades, we've been told not to brag about ourselves for fear of looking like shameless and obnoxious self-promoters. As I learned from an early age at The Registry Resort, doing a job well doesn't mean you will get noticed and get ahead. People around you need to gain awareness of who you are, your accomplishments and what your strengths are for your brand to gain traction.

Far too many people believe this means walking boldly into the CEO's office or a company meeting and shamelessly shoving others out of the way to announce your latest conquest. However, there is a distinct difference between bragging and sharing who you are.

"Conceit is bragging about yourself. Confidence means you believe you can get the job done," Johnny Unitas, legendary quarterback in the American National Football League.

Bragging crosses the line to conceit when you disregard other people for the sake of sharing your own victories, despite the circumstances around you.

On the other hand, when you choose to share yourself, your plans and your accomplishments, it is like letting people in on a good secret that they will get excited about and share with their friends.

Have you ever planned a surprise party?

Whether it is at an office with cupcakes to congratulate a successful sale or a birthday party with your best friend, it is exciting to think about and plan a good surprise party. First, you as the planner get excited about the end result: the surprised look and overwhelming joy of your friend. Then, as you realize that you need some help coordinating details like getting the person to the right spot or decorating the room without revealing the party, you start approaching friends and colleagues for support.

When you describe your plans for the party and how much fun it is going to be, how do they react? I've always found people love planning a party. It doesn't matter how much "real" work has to get done, they savor the opportunity to get out of their daily routine with something positive and inspiring.

Occasionally, you send updates to the planning group so they know that the conference room is booked, balloons ordered, and the perfect cake from the bakery is ordered - the chocolate cake with cherries - and of course the gluten-free and dairy-free dessert for Betty, too! As long as your updates aren't too frequent, they just add to the excitement and build anticipation for the group.

Even the people who don't directly help out love being in on the secret beforehand because it makes them feel as though they are in on something special. It lets them know that you think highly enough of them to bring them into the inner circle. They feel connected to you because you invited them and then they get to feel like a real member of the group at the party because they were a part of the planning.

Shouldn't your life be the same way? Why not make it as fun as planning a surprise party?

Think about what the party will look like, invite your friends to help in the planning and milestones, and share in the cake at the end of the day!

By sharing yourself during the branding process, you will build stronger relationships that can last a lifetime. And, at the end of the game, you will have a LOT of guests at the party to celebrate Brand [You]!

When you start looking for the right people to bring on board, think about sharing your plans and your accomplishments by:

- Choosing the right conversation starters

- Choosing the right time

- Choosing the right venue

- Choosing the right personal boundaries

What are the right conversation starters?

For millions of business professionals, the hardest part in starting a conversation is opening your mouth. How many opportunities have you lost simply because you were trying to think of the perfect opening line? Or, when someone approached you to start a conversation, you unconsciously replied with a closed-ended response like "Yes", "No", or "That was nice"?

The good news is that by working through the exercises in this book, you are already crafting your conversation starters, all the exciting plans and progress for Brand [You]. Go back to your top five accomplishments and your key messages for ideas.

Realize that sharing some of your exciting news doesn't need to be a lengthy conversation. The next time someone asks how you are doing, you can either answer:

"Pretty good" and quietly go about your day...

OR

"Great! I just wrapped up a project for XYZ client and they are thrilled! How are you doing?", and take two minutes to share yourself, genuinely show interest in a colleague and build your relationship.

> ### Conversation Starters That Reinforce Your Brand
>
> KEY MESSAGE - YOU ARE AN INFLUENCER OR [YOU]TOPIA
>
> *Response to "How Are you?"* - Great! You know, I'm not sure if you heard the news but I was just asked to speak at XYZ conference. It is so exciting to share my love of...
>
> *How does this response reinforce your brand?* - Congratulations! The conference organizers have just endorsed your expertise and influence.
>
> Letting your friends know how excited you are to share your passion allows them to get excited for you without feeling pressured to attend.

You've opened up a conversation by giving them enough information to ask for more. Or, allow them to gracefully continue on their day by saying congratulations and patting you on the back.

Key Message - Establish credibility with your top five accomplishments

Response to "How Are you?" - Great! Working with XYZ client is about to wrap up. This project has really pushed me to get out of my comfort zone and come up with some creative solutions. What a great learning opportunity to...

How does this response reinforce your brand? - Letting a colleague know whom you are working with "XYZ Client" is a co-branding statement. The fact that you are working with this client is an implied endorsement by the client and positions your brand alongside theirs. Make sure you choose clients you want to brand with.

Enthusiastically describing a creative solution gives you credibility as a professional who wants to learn and provide the right solutions for your clients.

You've opened up the opportunity for a conversation by giving them enough information to ask for more. And maybe you've inspired them to get out of their comfort zone with a client issue.

Key Message - Relevance and "What is in it for me" (WIIFM) through your benefits statements

Response to "How Are you?" - Great! I was just thinking about calling you. My friend "Fred" is helping me out on XYZ project... He's a great guy and he needs some advice about... Would you mind if I make an introduction and send your contact information?

How does this response reinforce your brand? - By taking a genuine interest in people through your Ideal Customers, Network of Peers and Inspirational Relationships, you are going to find that you have more opportunities to connect them.

Making a genuine and relevant referral is an endorsement of their skills and demonstrates your desire to help them make money, save time, or inspire action. The key to success is follow through on action or you risk killing your credibility.

You've opened up the opportunity for a conversation by giving them enough information to ask for more.

Key Message - Your brand value

Response to "How Are you?" - Great! I just came from a luncheon where one of my clients was recognized for their outstanding recycling program. They are a small business, so being promoted in front of such a large group is a huge employee morale booster and hopefully it will translate into some additional business!

How does this response reinforce your brand? - As you read earlier, brand value is about more than a consulting fee that you are charging. It is about understanding a client's needs and providing the right solutions.

This kind of response demonstrates that you are looking at the bigger picture of a business' success in terms of publicity, marketing, employee morale and the ultimate driver of paying customers. While you may offer a very specific consulting product, your ability to see how that affects the broader success of the company makes you infinitely more valuable.

You've opened up the opportunity for a conversation by giving them enough information to ask for more or make a graceful exit.

Key Message - What action would you like people to take?

Response to "How Are you?" - Great! Hey, I've been meaning to call you and ask for your advice. I know that you are active in Rotary and I'm looking for a way to connect with them about helping a non-profit that I volunteer for. Is there a committee or person that I can reach out to help make introductions?

How does this response reinforce your brand? - As a relationship builder, you are showing a genuine knowledge and interest in someone else's interests which elevates your brand.

> Your request co-brands you with the non-profit that you are volunteering for and allows for a mutual connection. Perhaps this contact is also a supporter of your non-profit organization?
>
> By asking for help in this kind way, you are inviting them to help plan the party without pressuring them to do something they aren't able to.
>
> You've opened up the opportunity for a conversation by giving them enough information to ask for more or follow up at a later date.

Keeping up-to-date lists of your projects and accomplishments is important to remember. But each day brings a reason to be proud. Every day has a milestone, no matter how small, that you've achieved toward [You]topia and Brand [You]. Keep a cheat sheet of conversation starters for a month or so, but you'll quickly find that the more important step is to open up your mind, open up your mouth, and just start talking.

When is the right time?

Waiting for the perfect time is often the perfect excuse to never do something. If you want to build awareness of who you are, what you are working on and what you have accomplished, dozens of small opportunities appear during the day to make that happen. As we described above, it can be as simple as a response to "How are you doing?"

Now, if you walk around your office spouting the same response to ten or fifteen people along the way, you are going to earn a reputation for over-sharing. So think strategically about the timing and change your answers slightly, so that you don't overshare like some people on Facebook.

What time of day are you fresh in your thinking? During this time, you will project a stronger and more confident version of Brand [You].

What time of day are you most receptive to listening to people and actively engaging in a conversation? If you are distracted from the conversation, you are just going to kill your credibility and look like a jerk. Pick a time during which you can engage.

What is your most productive time of day? We all have real tasks that need to be accomplished. Stay productive when that works best for you, then open up for conversations when you are more relaxed.

What time of day are your Ideal Customers, Network of Peers and Inspirational Relationships most available to engage in a conversation? Your brain may be freshest at 4 am, but you will certainly lose Brand Value if you start calling on customers who aren't awake that early!

I've found I am at my freshest and also most productive in the mornings. To manage my schedule, I try to book two to three breakfast meetings per month with energizing people. One of those meetings is a CEO breakfast in which I usually run into more than a dozen contacts who are equally open and ready to network.

I've also found that late afternoons are a terrible time for me to network. I start wrapping up the day's projects so that I can get home to spend time with my daughter. If you call me after 4 pm, be prepared for a short conversation. I also limit my evening networking events because my heart just isn't in it and I know that it shows. It is more beneficial for me to use that time to re-energize in other ways.

By picking the right time of day to share your accomplishments, you can take some of the pain and pressure out of networking. You'll be more confident in your delivery, your audience will be more receptive to hearing you, and Brand [You] will reap the benefits.

Where is the right venue?

Business professionals misguidedly think a press release is the only way to announce a promotion, certification, award or other accomplishment.

We often miss the smaller more intimate one-on-one conversations to share good news. It can be as simple as bumping into a colleague at the coffee machine or more strategically looking for prospects at the right networking groups.

I'm also a big fan of third-party endorsements. If you are too nervous to speak up about your own accomplishments at the next company meeting, take the opportunity to speak up about someone else.

It is easy to get caught up grinding through a meeting agenda and reviewing the standard facts, figures, sales strategies and all the other important need-to-know information while losing site of the more important reason to gather: building relationships.

Most agendas have at least five minutes set aside for new business. The next time your manager looks around the table and asks if anyone has new business to share, why not take the opportunity to share in the good news?

Get yourself a PR Buddy or two in the office to share in your accomplishments. Start it off by praising one of your colleagues...

- *"Jane may be too humble to share this, so I'm going to speak up for her. She just wrapped up a huge project for XYZ Customer ahead of schedule allowing them to move forward in their expansion. Way to go, Jane!"*

- *"One of my clients needed some extra help organizing a project. I knew Dick was an expert at this type of project, so I called him for extra backup. We worked as a team to take care of our client, who has now referred additional work our way. Awesome work, Dick!"*

> In my class of Leadership Collier whenever of our classmates makes the news, someone will send an email shout-out to all 45 of us. Inevitably, it sets off a string of reply-all emails where someone else will add in more good news. The abundance of emails earned us the nickname of the "Shameless Class", which we embraced wholeheartedly.
>
> Sometimes you read the emails and sometimes you chime in. But, when the email that sparks all of the replies is about you, it is a pretty special feeling.

Meetings also become more fun if you start with the good news, so maybe you could request five minutes at the beginning of the agenda to give a shout out to team members.

Keeping your boss "in-the-know" about your team's accomplishments makes you an invaluable resource. Most leaders understand the motivational power of public praise for a job well done. However, the hierarchal structure of an organization may leave them out of the loop on some of their best employees.

The CBS reality show "Undercover Boss" shows just how out of touch executives can be with their front-line employees. Well-intentioned CEOs have to don elaborate aliases to take on entry-level positions and get feedback from employees. Without the formality of their title, the executives are able to get much more honest feedback about the morale and accomplishments of their employees.

You don't have to recruit CBS to your company to open up the eyes of your executives. You can confidentially let them know about the good news and give them the opportunity to shine. Maybe when a customer writes a letter of recommendation? Or when a team member does something well? Or even when you earn a special accreditation or certification?

Email the good news to your boss with a note that says, "Just wanted to make sure you saw this letter of recommendation that came in from our client. Maybe it is worth mentioning at the next meeting?"

If you are an independent consultant, you can also partner with a PR Buddy in one of your networking groups, with an executive who likes to forward good news through executive boards and committees, or a friend who reposts good news on social networks such as LinkedIn and Facebook. This third party endorsement builds credibility and takes you off the hook for bragging about yourself.

Identify the influencers in your network who can help share your news and keep them in the loop!

Of course, there is always room for a press release to announce significant accomplishments. If you are in a corporate environment, you have to negotiate the politics of when and how to send out a press release. Always consult with your supervisor and the public relations department before sending something out on your own.

However, if you are an entrepreneur, consultant or an independent agent who is responsible for your own marketing and public relations, you have more options to publicly promote yourself. Either hire a public relations professional or learn how to write a press release to announce major accomplishments in every industry publication that your Ideal Customers read.

Smart Corporate Brands Speak Up About Their Employees

Culturally, we've seen a drastic shift in how national corporate brands interact in their local communities and Waste Management is a great example of a company that gets it right.

Waste Management is the leading provider of comprehensive waste management services in North America. It is the nation's largest recycler and a leading developer of waste-to-energy and landfill gas-to-energy facilities.

As a Fortune 200 company, Waste Management has a small corporate communications department responsible for developing, maintaining and protecting their corporate brand. The company looks for ways to serve the environmental needs of its customers, include providing zero waste solutions.

However, at the front line, the organization encourages employees to be role models of the brand through community involvement. By supporting the efforts of their employees and publicly praising them in the media, Waste Management is not just "promoting corporate talking points", the company seeks to demonstrate its brand value and key messages through proudly engaged employees.

"As one of the nation's leading environmental solutions providers, Waste Management engages employees to embrace the opportunity to 'Think Green Everyday' and carry that message into their communities through participating in volunteer community clean ups, school recycling programs and non-profit organizations that benefit our local environment," said Dawn McCormick, Manager Community Affairs, Waste Management Inc. of Florida.

The anatomy of a standard business press release announcement:

- Headline should be short and to the point

- Two body paragraphs should give the who, what, when, where and why it is important

- Last paragraph should be a boilerplate message about your company that includes "For more information, call (555) 555-5555, or visit www.YourWebsite.com"

Drafting a press release with too many irrelevant details is a mistake. If an editor has to struggle to get to the point, the press release will be abandoned and replaced by one of the thousand other releases that came in that day.

MEDIA ADVISORY

Chuck Greus named Outstanding Volunteer of 2012 by Keep Charlotte Beautiful

FOR MORE INFORMATION

Charlotte County, FL - March 25, 2013 - Keep Charlotte Beautiful is pleased to announce Chuck Greus, Customer Relations Manager for Waste Management of Charlotte County, as its Outstanding Volunteer of 2012.

Waste Management
Media
Dawn McCormick
(954) 226-9894
dmccormick@wm.com

Cyndee Woolley, APR
(239) 571-3174
cyndee@c2-com.com

During its 11th anniversary celebration, Keep Charlotte Beautiful recognized the efforts of the 4,156 volunteers and many business partnerships that donated 15,810 hours of service in 2012. With these partners, the non-profit organization is able to continue its mission of keeping the community clean and free of debris, beautifying neighborhood and public spaces, as well as instill a sense of pride and ownership for residents to protect the county's natural resources.

"As a non-profit organization, our greatest asset is our network of volunteers, private businesses and government partnerships. But, some like Chuck Greus, exceed our expectations," said Glenda Anderson, Executive Director for Keep Charlotte Beautiful.

Chuck Greus was recognized as the Outstanding Volunteer of 2012 for his assistance throughout the year. Providing logistical support, Greus helped facilitate multiple cleanup projects by coordinating waste collection services. Additionally, he volunteered on the beautification projects at The South County Park, Community Garden, the Girl Scout House, and the Parkside Community Garden.

About Keep Charlotte Beautiful
Keep Charlotte Beautiful helps improve the quality of life in Charlotte County through enhanced community awareness, education, and public/private partnerships. During the year, Keep Charlotte Beautiful partners with community organizations on the Great American Cleanup, Coastal Cleanup, Think Green Golf Tournament, Adopt-a-Road, Adopt-a-Highway, Adopt-a-Shore, Cigarette Prevention and the KCB Student Calendar Art Contest. For more information on how you can help, visit www.KeepCharlotteBeautiful.org.

About Waste Management
Waste Management, Inc., based in Houston, Texas, is the leading provider of comprehensive waste management services in North America. Through its subsidiaries, the company provides collection, transfer, recycling and resource recovery, and disposal services. It is one of the largest residential recyclers and also a leading developer, operator and owner of waste-to-energy and landfill gas-to-energy facilities in the United States. The company's customers include residential, commercial, industrial, and municipal customers throughout North America. To learn more information about Waste Management visit www.wm.com or www.thinkgreen.com.

What is the right amount of information to share?

As a business owner or business professional, you have a personality that gives you character, but if it goes into extremes, your personality could run the risk of offending a potential customer and losing business.

That is a valid concern because, at the end of the day, we are all in business to make money. It isn't about corporate greed; when we make money we have the ability to pay employees, donate to charities, purchase goods that further stimulate the economy.

Brand [You] defines how much personality you let spill out in your professional life. But, remember that building your brand isn't about creating a fake personality to sell yourself. Building Brand [You] is about living out your authentic self and leveraging your personality to stand out from the crowd.

In Southwest Florida, we have an abundance of University of Florida alumni, true Gator super fans who live and breathe their alma mater's orange and blue. Many of these alumni are business owners who choose to:

- Support their team on the weekends without advertising the fact that they are Gators.

  - Pros: If you are a casual fan, or you need to appeal to a broader audience of Ideal Customers, this could be the right strategy for you.

  - Cons: If your Ideal Customers share in your love of all things Gator, you might be missing out on a personal connection. You'll need to find another way to make your brand stand out.

- Support their team and show their pride by incorporating orange and blue into company colors to show their bond without going over the top.

    - Pros: This strategy is more appropriate if some of your Ideal Customers or referral sources are also Gators and you want to show the mutual connection.

    - Cons: This is a subtle strategy and doesn't necessarily leverage your passion to create a lasting impression. You'll need to find another way to make your brand stand out.

- Support their team AND leverage their passion for all things orange and blue by belonging to the local UF Alumni Association, networking with their Gator fans, coordinating tailgating parties, fishing trips and golf tournaments to engage their peers.

    - Pros: By being the "Super Fan" that is the center of influence, you can supplement your brand with something you love doing that will leave a lasting personal impression.

    - Cons: You might not win over any Florida State University customers, *but who needs them, anyway?*

But how can that personal impression really lead to more business with Brand [You]?

Politics and religion used to be taboo subjects to discuss at work, but one well-known football player has stood out from thousands of other players on the field by incorporating his faith and values into his personal brand.

Tim Tebow has been widely recognized as one of the greatest college football players of his time and perhaps the most expressive about his Christian beliefs.

In his career as a University of Florida (UF) Gator, he led the team to two national championships and was honored as the first sophomore recipient of the Heisman Trophy.

His skills on the field led him to be a first round draft pick by the Denver Broncos, where he led the franchise to the 2011 NFL Playoffs for the first time in six years. Although 2012 left Tebow unexpectedly benched most of the season for the New York Jets, his brand lives on precisely because he chose to be so open about his inspirational faith.

That choice to be so public certainly offended some people, but ultimately it built a brand and attracted attention that has allowed him to do so much more off the field, like write a book, capitalize on speaking opportunities, and provide a great deal of charitable support through the Tim Tebow Foundation. His brand set him apart from thousands of other football players who were likely as talented. He hasn't just made money for himself; he has energized Christians around the world and won over the hearts of millions of fans who never cared about football in the first place.

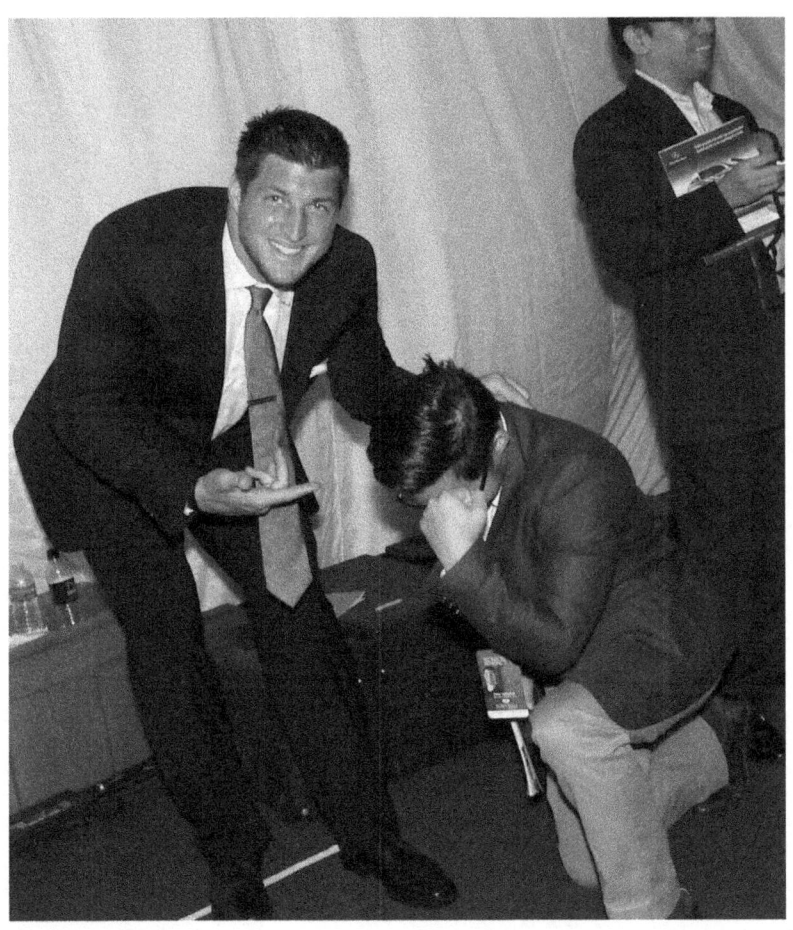

Photo by Reagan Rule, courtesy of Naples Town Hall Distinguished Speaker Series.

Daniel and Trisha Price wedding, December 31, 2011.

How different would his story be if he had chosen to play it safe and quietly conceal his faith?

When you have a dilemma about how much information to share, you can always go back to your five key messages and use them as a benchmark to cut through the clutter and decide, is this something that helps my brand? Or is this just extra information that people don't really need to know?

1) You are an influencer with a strong vision of where you are going in life with your [You]topia

2) Establish credibility with your top five accomplishments

3) Relevance and "What is in it for me" (WiiFM) through your benefits statements

4) Your brand value

5) What action do you want people to take?

"The future of all branding is personal. It is impossible to have a relationship with two distinct people - at work and at home. Embrace your brand and build stronger relationships," said Andrew Davis, author of "Brandscaping".

As a business owner, should you encourage your employees to develop a personal brand?

Many executives are concerned about losing talent. It is expensive to recruit, train and maintain employees.

However, if you are focusing your efforts on defensively protecting your employees, you are limiting yourself as a manager whose role is reduced to simply putting out fires. A true leader seeks to build a culture in which the staff wants to be a part of a winning team and to help achieve the company's goals.

Today's employees are motivated by personal growth and opportunity. As you help them learn and choose the right career path, two categories of employees will become clear. Some will become more and more loyal to you and your mission; others will fall off because they aren't the right fit. Either way, you've built a stronger company culture with a team that is dedicated to moving toward the same company mission.

"You will probably grow smart people that will eventually outgrow you, but you can do it in a way that helps your company instead of hurting it," said Andrew Davis, author of "Brandscaping".

"If you don't get noticed, you don't have anything. You just have to be noticed, but the art is in getting noticed naturally, without screaming or without tricks," Leo Burnett, founder of Leo Burnett Worldwide.

YOUR NOTES

CHAPTER THIRTEEN

7. BE RELEVANT OR BE REPLACEABLE

The emergence of the Millennial Generation sent shock waves through the marketing world, as brands and corporations struggled to keep up and understand this elusive generation, born between 1979 and the early 2000s. While the opinions about the precise birth year of this group varies from company to company, they are an overwhelming force of 80 to100 million consumers who are actively influencing the lives of millions of older and younger people.

As digital natives, they don't remember life without a remote control, computers, and smartphones. Their lives have been filled with mass customization. While previous generations have remained loyal to brands, Millennials crave variety and options. They are passionate about social change and preserving the environment.

So, how are the nation's largest brands staying relevant to this massive customer group?

Over the past decade, the country's largest fast food chain has responded to its evolving customer demands by offering healthier side dishes, more appealing salads and a line of affordable premium beverages with the McCafe.

In addition to nutritional improvements, the company has made increasing efforts to build a sustainable supply chain and reduce carbon impact by using more energy-efficient equipment in their restaurants. In 2013, McDonald's launched the Premium McWrap, a more customizable sandwich with a fresh lineup of vegetables and sauces.

With a less customizable product line, Coke has maintained market share with Millennials by working to build relationships across social-media platforms and appealing to the generation's sense of individuality through their interests, such as music and gadgets.

In 2010, Gatorade launched its Mission Control center to monitor social networks and engage in one-on-one conversations with consumers. According to an *AdAge* article, Mission Control is credited with increased mentions of the signature product "G Series Pro" and, from an industry perspective, increased discussions about sports performance to nearly 60 percent, from 35 percent, in six short months. [15]

At the beginning of this book, you went through your own evaluation to gain perspective on your brand and how people perceive you *(Chapter 4)*. To stay relevant, you need to continue to evaluate Brand [You] and the outside circumstances to make sure you stay on track, moving toward [You]topia.

Listen and take action

Fortunately, you don't have to set up your own Mission Control center to get a pulse on your own brand. It can be as simple as listening in at the proverbial cocktail party.

Josh Miles had been underestimating the brand he had cultivated until he overheard a conversation at a networking group where someone was describing Miles Design, "They [Miles Design] do really high-end professional work."

His marketing and branding company had carved out a specialty niche working with technically oriented clients such as engineers, architects and accountants. Miles hadn't considered his company serving a premium customer, but he took the opportunity to capitalize on what the market was already saying about his company to elevate his brand.

Joe Pulizzi stumbled into a brand element during a post-lecture meet and greet. Pulizzi had unknowingly worn the color bright orange - in different ways - at a few speaking engagements. It left an impression with the audience because, when they described him to friends, they said, "You can't miss Joe. He is the guy with a lot of energy and he'll be wearing orange."

When Pulizzi wore a black suit one day, a lecture attendee became concerned and asked if he was feeling okay. From that day forward, he wore orange to every speaking engagement. And the orange continues to multiply as people send him orange Legos, shoes, ties, and desktop gifts.

Develop your own Brain Trust

Executives worldwide tap into coaches and peer groups to hone their decision-making and get honest, actionable feedback. Coaching and peer groups have risen dramatically in popularity in the past five years, despite the tightening of the economy at all levels.

Peer groups take many forms, but the basic structure is built around a group of non-competing businesses that attend formal meetings, which are lead, by a trained facilitator or coach. During the meetings, the executives may learn about industry topics and best practices or time is dedicated to problem or issue discussion within a confidential setting.

The success of the group depends on the facilitator's ability to keep the conversations moving as well as the synergy and dedication of the members. While many top-level executives find the structure useful, some of us (myself included) are more comfortable opening up in a one-on-one setting, rather than a group setting. If you are an entrepreneur, manager, or an emerging executive, the significant financial and time investment of a formal peer group might also be prohibitive.

Fortunately, because you've been working to build your own Network of Peers, you can easily build your own Brain Trust to help your brand grow and thrive.

1) Go back and review your top five career goals that will get you to [You]topia. Write them on the Top 5 Career Goals Worksheet on page 186.

2) Review your Network of Peers and identify one person who can help you achieve your goals, either because he or she has already achieved these goals, or is an expert in the industry, or by sheer motivational force will hold you accountable for these goals. This person should be a trusted source who will maintain confidentiality. Perhaps you have to offer, as well?

3) In this Brain-Trust relationship, what do you hope to achieve from the relationship? As we've discussed in several chapters, clutter and disorder will only leave you discussing issues instead of taking action.

Processing issues

For your (free) Brain Trust to be effective, you have to respect each other's time. Processing issues or opportunities can be distilled into a lunchtime conversation or less. Using this formula forces you to cut through the clutter and prepare for action after you make a decision.

I. What is the core problem or opportunity and why is this important to you?

II. What are the contributing factors in terms of budget, job structure, time, resources?

III. What are three options you could take?

   a. Do nothing and let the problem/opportunity resolve itself

   b. Do something to mitigate the problem/capitalize on the opportunity with minimal resources

   c. Commit yourself and all available resources to this

IV. What are the most significant risks/rewards?

V. What is your next follow-up action step?

Ongoing feedback

With an established relationship, it is much easier to pick up the phone and talk more casually about the general pulse of the industry and your brand. Some of my executive clients have taken the route of a weekly coffee appointment, a monthly lunch or regular phone call.

The important thing is to let each other know what you are hoping to achieve by simply stating something like, "I would like to schedule a regular time to chat with you about how our businesses are going so that we can help each other stay ahead of the competition."

Then you have to keep your relationship close enough to know what is going on in each other's businesses. If you start missing too many appointments, you will lose all perspective on what kind of advice would be appropriate.

It might also help you to have a list of open-ended questions for your conversations. You can easily type these into a recurring appointment on your calendar so that you can quickly reference them.

- What project are you working on this week?

- What do you find most challenging about this project?

- What did you learn about this project?

- Is this having a positive/negative impact on your brand?

- Have you heard anything in the community/industry that you think is important for me?

4) Be open to receiving honest feedback. As much as we like to think that we are open to receiving honest feedback, that "openness" is generally more reserved for positive feedback. Criticism is much harder to take, even when it is constructive criticism.

Think about the last time someone offered you criticism. Maybe it was your boss, spouse or a friend. Did you get instantly defensive because the person didn't understand all of the circumstances about why you made that decision? Did you dismiss the comments or think about them later when your head was clear? Did you make any changes?

We've all been caught off guard and reacted defensively to criticism. But, if "defensive" or "poor listener" are a part of your brand right now, it will be a lot harder for you to get constructive feedback.

When you start establishing your Brain Trust, sit back and ask open-ended questions. Let your Brain Trust members know that you genuinely want to hear the truth about your brand. Open yourself up by disclosing a concern or an issue and let them into your world. Be prepared for some awkward silence in the beginning, but as the relationship grows you will both benefit from the dialogue.

5) Stay accountable to yourself. Staying relevant and staying in touch is ultimately your responsibility. If you lose touch with your Brain Trust, they will move on to their own projects and work within their own circle of influence to achieve their own goals.

At best, you lose focus and momentum on Brand [You].

At worst, you begin to lose credibility and have to repair Brand [You].

Schedule the time in your calendar and make it happen.

TOP 5 CAREER GOALS WORKSHEET

Goal 1: _____

One expert I know that can help me achieve this goal is: _____

With this relationship, I hope to achieve: _____

Goal 2: _____

One expert I know that can help me achieve this goal is: _____

With this relationship, I hope to achieve: _____

Goal 3: _____

One expert I know that can help me achieve this goal is: _____

With this relationship, I hope to achieve: _____

Goal 4: _____

One expert I know that can help me achieve this goal is: _____

With this relationship, I hope to achieve: _____

Goal 5: _____

One expert I know that can help me achieve this goal is: _____

With this relationship, I hope to achieve: _____

Focusing on your end-goal will make your brand strong. But, regularly listening for and responding to the market conditions as well as constructive feedback will make your brand stronger. Take the time to tap into the valuable human resources that you have readily available in your Network of Peers.

Find a mentor who is where you want to be in ten years

People who are truly passionate about what they do will be more than willing to help you do it even better.

In 2005, Felix Baumgartner set out to break the sound barrier during the Red Bull Stratos project. Jumping from an estimated 39 kilometers above Earth was also going to shatter the 45+-year record of Col. Joseph William Kittinger's 31-kilometer skydive in 1960.

Instead of creating an adversarial competition, Baumgartner reached out to Col. Kittinger and asked him to join the crew and mentor him through the process. In 2012, when the jump was completed, Col. Kittinger was the capsule communicator, directing Baumgartner on his record-breaking freefall.

When asked how it felt to have Col. Kittinger working on the project, Baumgartner replied, "I want to inspire the next generation. As I sit here next to Joe Kittinger in this press conference, I'm hoping that in 40 years there will be someone asking my advice because he wants to break my records."

YOUR NOTES

CHAPTER FOURTEEN

Conclusion

Whether you are building a corporate empire like Donald Trump, pursuing peace like Gandhi, starting a computer revolution like Steve Jobs, or breaking the sound barrier like Felix Baumgartner, it all begins with a dream and a vision for the future.

Building a personal brand is about much more than pinning your reputation on hope, a dream and a fashionable accessory.

It is about:

- Cutting out the clutter and distractions so that you can focus in on what is most important and fulfilling in your life.

- Creating a passionate vision of [You]topia, so that you stay energized and motivated on your path.

- Identifying the core essence of who you are, where you are going and how you are going to get there.

- Recognizing your own accomplishments and strengths so that you can easily convey your brand value in short, simple key messages.

- Developing relationships that help you generate income, stay relevant and keep you personally inspired so that you can live out your wildest dreams.

Many people have the most amazing dreams of what they "could" do, but they get caught up in the distractions and immediate needs of everyday life. They are so busy dealing with tasks and getting through the day, they forget to live out their dreams.

By taking the time to build Brand [You], you will stand out from the crowd by creating a detailed branding strategy that puts you on a direct path to your dreams.

7 Lessons in building Brand [You]

1. You are Brand [You]

Building Brand [You] is vital to achieving your own personal success. It is about finding a clear direction, getting feedback and honing the message about who you are and what you offer.

Distractions from the everyday clutter of life bombard us all. But, by taking the time to focus or refocus your brand, you are taking the first step in transforming your personal brand into something more meaningful to you and making yourself more relevant in today's world.

2. Set your sights and your goals for [You]topia

So many people fail to think through their goals, leaving their life path to be cluttered up and distracted by what other people think are the right goals.

By taking the time to consider exactly what your [You]topia is and aligning your values and priorities, you will be able to clearly see the right path for you and run unbridled, full speed ahead.

3. Value Brand [You] or no one else will

Your brand is a promise to deliver exactly what a customer needs, when he or she needs it. That value is determined by your vision of the future and by a clear understanding of your Ideal Customer and why they value your services.

Gimmicks and promotions may attract attention, but they are more likely to detract from your real brand value and undercut your business. By focusing your efforts on consistently delivering exactly what your brand promises to targeted customers who trust you, you will build a much stronger clientele and profit margin.

4. Build your network wisely

Building your network of Ideal Customers, Network of Peers and Inspirational Contacts is about strategically organizing and prioritizing your relationships.

Millions of people roam aimlessly through life, without the dedication or desire to commit to their own success. Unfortunately, they often pop up during inopportune times and try to pull you off your path. Fortunately, there are millions more people who are just like you, who want to lift you up and help you succeed.

By organizing your contacts into Ideal Customers, a solid Network of Peers and Inspirational Relationships that keep you motivated, you can focus your efforts and energy on the right relationships.

5. Brand [You] must be simple, short and strong

You must describe your brand in a way that engages people from the beginning. First impressions matter and they happen in the blink of an eye.

With your brand in place, you can make conscious choices to deliver the key messages that will help you succeed. The first impressions that you make should convey confidence and a solid sense of direction--from being appropriately dressed to refining your body language so that you are approachable.

Here's what your key messages must project:

1) You are an influencer because you have a vivid vision of your [You]topia

2) Establish credibility with your top five accomplishments

3) Relevance and "What is in it for me" (WiiFM) through your benefits statements

4) Your brand value

6) What action do you want people to take?

At the end of the day, how you make people feel about your brand creates the strong emotional connection. While you have to make sure that you are sending the right message, you also have to tune into the messages other people are sending back and respond appropriately. Your response will build trust and complete the relationship.

6. Smart brands speak up

Doing a job well doesn't mean that you will get noticed. Be cautious about getting noticed in a positive way. You don't want to be the office jerk that shoves other people out of the way to pursue your own agenda.

Fortunately, there are many ways to speak up and share your good news so that people feel as if they are "in" on a good secret. Most people, and certainly the most important people in your life, want to share in your success.

Look for the smaller opportunities in the day to share your good news. When someone asks how you are doing, let them know just how excited you are about a new project, a new committee, a new client, or just share a positive smile with a co-worker.

When you have really good news, take the time to issue a press release so that your Network of Peers and the business community recognize your accomplishments and see you as the passionate influencer that you are.

Speaking up enables you to build a strong relationship with people who understand the value of your brand and who will consistently refer the right kind of customers who will drive your growth.

7. Be relevant or be replaceable

Staying relevant to your Ideal Customers is crucial for any brand to thrive. As a brand with a strong and passionate vision for the future, you can stay true to your core values and priorities while adjusting your approach to stay relevant to your existing customers while attracting the next generation.

Smart brands start with listening. Listen for feedback from your Ideal Customers, Network of Peers and even Inspirational Relationships to make sure the brand message you think you are sending is the one that is actually getting through. Or, perhaps like Josh Miles whose brand evolved to "really high-end", your brand will become more valuable than you ever imagined.

Taking feedback one step further, develop a Brain Trust - either formal or informal - to get regular, honest, actionable feedback. By taking your top five goals and identifying one person who is a trusted expert that can offer you advice, you'll be more likely to achieve and exceed your own goals. Before you contact your expert resource, make sure you have processed your goal and know what you really hope to get out of the relationship.

It is time to build Brand [You]

As you've learned in this book, this new age of personal branding is much more than a mark on a piece of paper or a creative company name. Your brand is a the total sum of a person's experience with you - whether you create that experience intentionally or let it happen inadvertently.

Now is the time to invest in yourself by building Brand [You]. Take the time to develop your brand so that you stand out from the crowd with a strategy that puts you on a direct path to your dreams.

Be Relevant
Be [You]

YOUR NOTES

ACKNOWLEDGEMENTS

When you surround yourself by great people, the only way to go is up. I am so grateful for the ongoing support of my family, friends and clients who have all encouraged me to pursue my dreams.

Special thanks to...

My friend and colleague Jessica Macera, who has spent the last two years helping develop and hone the Brand [You] process.

My Brand [You] Brain Trust who gave the final book thoughtful review and constructive criticism. Thanks to Judy Bricker, Russell Budd, Anne Frazier, Jim Molenaar and Mario Valle!

Mollie Page Griffin, a true friend who has always been there to cheer me on or kick me back on the right track.

And of course, my publisher and friend Newt Barrett with Voyager Media, Inc. for his patience, guidance and assistance through this process.

ABOUT THE AUTHOR

Cyndee Woolley, APR, is an award winning public relations, branding and community outreach consultant with a demonstrated track record of campaigns that generate results. She was a key team member in a public awareness campaign that resulted in the successful negotiation of a contract valued at $210 million dollars for Waste Management.

Passionate about advancing her industry, Woolley has led training initiatives in branding, public relations and social media for businesses, non-profit organizations and universities. She has also served as a leader in the Public Relations Society of America (PRSA), where she was elected the 2013 Chair of the Sunshine District.

Woolley believes in giving back to the community by taking an active role in professional and civic organizations. In recent years, she has volunteered on marketing and branding committies for The Shelter for Abused Women and Children, Naples Equestrian Challenge, and the Leadership Collier Foundation. She is also a past-chair of the Farm City BBQ, a non-profit organization that brings nearly 1,500 business and agricultural leaders together and raises money for youth leadership development.

REFERENCES

Chapter 1

1. American Banker, "Women Hold the Key to Their Career", September, 14, 2012. http://www.americanbanker.com/news/alberta-cefis-discusses-keys-women-career-advancement-1052682-1.html?pg=2&wib

Chapter 3

2. National First Ladies' Library, "First Lady Biography: Hillary Clinton", Retrieved Jan 03, 2013 from http://www.firstladies.org/biographies/firstladies.aspx?biography=43

3. Lady Gaga. (2013). The Biography Channel website. Retrieved 09:09, Jan 03, 2013, from http://www.biography.com/people/lady-gaga-481598

4. Al Gore, "Tim Cook", Time Magazine's The World's 100 Most Influential People: 2012, April 18, 2012. http://www.time.com/time/specials/packages/article/0,28804,2111975_2111976_2112101,00.html

5. Tim Cook. (2013). *The Biography Channel website*. Retrieved 12:20, May 01, 2013, from http://www.biography.com/people/tim-cook-20967297

Chapter 5

6. Mike Michalowicz, "7 Habits of the World's Best Business Leaders", Open Forum, October 2, 2012. http://www.openforum.com/articles/7-habits-of-the-worlds-best-business-leaders

Chapter 6

7. Greg McKeown, "If you Don't Prioritize Your Life, Someone Else Will", Harvard Business Review, June 2012. http://blogs.hbr.org/cs/2012/06/how_to_say_no_to_a_controlling.html

Chapter 7

8. Jonah Sachs, "How to Create a Brand with Values", FastCoexist.com, 2012. http://www.fastcoexist.com/1679967/how-to-create-a-brand-with-values

9. Tony Hsieh, "Your Culture is Your Brand", Huff Post Business, November 17, 2010. http://www.huffingtonpost.com/tony-hsieh/zappos-founder-tony-hsieh_1_b_783333.html

Chapter 10

10. Nike case study - Center for Applied Research http://www.cfar.com/Documents/nikecmp.pdf

11. Ellen Florian, ÈTony Hsieh: The best advice I ever got, È Fortune, May 1, 2012. http://money.cnn.com/2012/04/30/technology/best-advice-zappos-hsieh.fortune.htm

Chapter 11

12. Ben and Kelly Decker, "The Top Ten Best (and Worst) Communicators of 2012", December 18, 2012. http://decker.com/blog/the-top-ten-best-and-worst-communicators-of-2012

13. Steve Jobs' Commencement Speech, Stanford Report, June 14, 2005. http://news.stanford.edu/news/2005/june15/jobs-061505.html

14. "Oprah Talks to Ralph Lauren", *O, The Oprah Magazine,* October 2002. http://www.oprah.com/omagazine/Oprah-Interviews-Ralph-Lauren/10#ixzz2Niyx3X4c

Chapter 13

15. Natalie Zmuda, "Inside Gatorade's Social Media 'Mission Control'", AdvertisingAge, September 28, 2010. http://adage.com/article/news/video-inside-gatorade-s-social-media-mission-control/146149

www.ingramcontent.com/pod-product-compliance
Lightning Source LLC
Chambersburg PA
CBHW061305110426
42742CB00012BA/2057